INNOVATION
POLICY
SPAIN

ORGANISATION FOR ECONOMIC CO-OPERATION AND DEVELOPMENT

Pursuant to article 1 of the Convention signed in Paris on 14th December, 1960, and which came into force on 30th September, 1961, the Organisation for Economic Co-operation and Development (OECD) shall promote policies designed:

- to achieve the highest sustainable economic growth and employment and a rising standard of living in Member countries, while maintaining financial stability, and thus to contribute to the development of the world economy;
- to contribute to sound economic expansion in Member as well as non-member countries in the process of economic development; and
- to contribute to the expansion of world trade on a multilateral, non-discriminatory basis in accordance with international obligations.

The original Member countries of the OECD are Austria, Belgium, Canada, Denmark, France, the Federal Republic of Germany, Greece, Iceland, Ireland, Italy, Luxembourg, the Netherlands, Norway, Portugal, Spain, Sweden, Switzerland, Turkey, the United Kingdom and the United States. The following countries acceded subsequently through accession at the dates hereafter: Japan (28th April, 1964), Finland (28th January, 1969), Australia (7th June, 1971) and New Zealand (29th May, 1973).

The Socialist Federal Republic of Yugoslavia takes part in some of the work of the OECD (agreement of 28th October, 1961).

Publié en français sous le titre:

LA POLITIQUE D'INNOVATION
ESPAGNE

This report is the third in the series of Reviews of National Innovation Policy.

These reviews of innovation policy have two purposes: first, to enable the countries concerned to appraise the political, economic and structural aspects of the action taken to reinforce the role of technological innovation in the achievement of national goals.

Secondly, the reviews help to enrich the pool of available knowledge on the content of innovation policies and their role as an instrument of government. In this way OECD Member and non-Member countries can derive lessons which will help them to perfect their own scientific and technical set-up and improve their methods. Similarly, through this improved knowledge of the resources deployed by Member countries, the reviews help to strengthen international co-operation in the field of innovation stimulation policies.

Although each review is mainly centred on the specific problems of the country under review, there is a common procedure for preparing and conducting them. The process of review consists of the following stages:

- The preparation by the OECD Secretariat or by the country under review of a Background Report.
- An information mission: a team of Examiners visits the country under review and contacts those responsible for innovation policy, and the representatives of those which it is designed for: officials, industrialists, and academics. The Examiners also visit a certain number of firms, laboratories, universities and public institutions. The aim of this second stage is to supplement the information provided by the Background Report and to enable the Examiners to formulate, as a first approximation, what they deem to be the main problems raised by the implementation of the innovation policy under review: this constitutes the Examiners' Report.
- The presentation, after appropriate revision, of the two reports to the OECD Committee for Scientific and Technological Policy. In the case of the Review of the Innovation Policy of Spain, these reports are presented in a single volume; for some countries the two reports may in fact be merged.

The members of the team of Examiners were: Mr. Pierre Piganiol (Rapporteur), Former Délégué à la Recherche (France); Mr. Konrad Ratz, Director, Fund for Research Promotion, Vienna (Austria); Mr. Benjamin Huberman, Former Deputy Director of the Office for Scientific and Technological Policy at the White House (USA). For the OECD Secretariat, Mrs M. Solanes co-ordinated the review and, with Mr. J.E. Aubert, took part in the Examiners' visit in May 1985.

Also Available

EVALUATION OF RESEARCH. A Selection of Current Practices (July 1987)
(92 87 05 1) ISBN 92-64-12981-2   78 pages   £5.00   US$11.00   F50.00   DM22.00

INNOVATION POLICY.   IRELAND (March 1987)
(92 87 01 1) ISBN 92-64-12918-9   76 pages   £5.00   US$10.00   F50.00   DM22.00

INNOVATION POLICY.   FRANCE (February 1987)
(92 86 06 1) ISBN 92-64-12884-0   296 pages   £16.00 US$32.00   F160.00 DM71.00

INNOVATION POLICY.   WESTERN PROVINCES OF CANADA
To be pusblished

STI - SCIENCE TECHNOLOGY INDUSTRY REVIEW

No. 1/Autumn 1986 (January 1987)
(90 86 01 1) ISBN 92-64-128888-3   129 pages

No. 2/September 1987
(90 87 01 1) ISBN 92-64-13002-0   174 pages

Per issue: £8.00   US$16.00   F80.00   DM35.00
1987 Subscription (No. 2 & No. 3 1987):   £15.00 US$30.00   F150.00 DM66.00

REVIEWS OF NATIONAL SCIENCE AND TECHNOLOGY POLICY:

NETHERLANDS (August 1987)
(92 87 03 1) ISBN 92-64-12955-3-3   142 pages   £9.50   US$20.00   F95.00   DM35.00

SWEDEN (June 1987)
(92 87 04 1) ISBN 92-64-12958-8   112 pages   £6.00   US$13.00   F60.00   DM26.00

FINLAND (April 1987)
(92 87 02 1) ISBN 92-64-6412928-6   154 pages   £9.50   US$19.00   F95.00   DM42.00

AUSTRALIA (August 1986)
(92 86 05 1) ISBN 92-64-12851-4   120 pages   £7.50   US$15.00   F75.00   DM33.00

PORTUGAL (June 1986)
(92 86 04 1) ISBN 92-64-12840-9   136 pages   £8.00   US$16.00   F80.00   DM35.00

RECOMBINANT DNA SAFETY CONSIDERATIONS. Safety Considerations for Industrial, Agricultural and Environmental Applications of Organisms Derived by Recombinant DNA Techniques (September 1986)
(93 86 02 1) ISBN 92-64-12857-3   70 pages   £6.00   US$12.00   F60.00   DM27.00

BIOTECHNOLOGY AND PATENT PROTECTION. An International Review by F.K. Beier, R.S. Crespi and J. Straus (September 1985)
(93 85 05 1) ISBN 92-64-12757-7   134 pages   £8.00   US$16.00   F80.00   DM35.00

Price charged at the OECD Bookshop.

THE OECD CATALOGUE OF PUBLICATIONS and supplements will be sent free of charge on request addressed either to OECD Publications Service, Sales and Distribution Division, 2, rue André-Pascal, 75775 PARIS CEDEX 16, or to the OECD Sales Agent in your country.

TABLE OF CONTENTS

Part I
GENERAL REPORT

Part II
EXAMINERS' REPORT

Part III

ACCOUNT OF THE REVIEW MEETING

LIST OF TABLES

LIST OF FIGURES

The Examiners and the Directorate for Science, Technology and Industry of the OECD desire to express their warmest thanks to the Spanish authorities and the many eminent Spanish personalities whose contribution has made possible this study of Spanish Innovation Policy.

It would be impossible to thank personally all those who helped in this exercise in Spain. They wish, however, to express their particular gratitude to all government departments and agencies who through the examination process have allowed the Examiners and the Secretariat to supplement their information and to gain a better understanding of the problems associated with Innovation Policy in Spain. The Directorate for Industrial Innovation and Technology of the Ministry for Industry must receive special thanks for its valuable help throughout the review and for having organised the Examiners' stay in Spain.

They would also like to thank the representatives of the universities, the industries and the various non-profit institutions who have not spared any effort to make this exercise a success.

The Examiners and the Secretariat were most appreciative of the open-mindedness and liberal spirit of the officials they met while conducting the survey.

BACKGROUND AND SUMMARY

General context of the Report

The Spanish economy is currently passing through an important process of adaptation. Not so long ago, Spain was the world's tenth most important industrial power. Now, like other OECD countries, she is obliged to convert and adapt her industry, establishing new activities in place of those in decline, such as steelmaking, shipbuilding, textiles and others. Although her entry into the Common Market will certainly assist her eventual integration into the international economy, its immediate effect will be to subject many sectors – particularly agriculture – to new pressures and strains.

The process of adaptation has already led to increased unemployment, which in 1984 reached an average of 20 per cent of the working population, being in some regions much greater and a cause of considerable anxiety. Again as in other OECD countries, this unemployment is particularly severe among young people (in 1983, 42 per cent of those out of work were under 25 years old).

The country's economic adaptation is taking place in a general context of progressive modernisation of political and administrative structures. The establishment of parliamentary democracy, which began ten years ago, has opened up new perspectives: a process of regionalisation, marked by the restoration of the old self-governing communities and the creation of new ones, is providing opportunities for some very interesting developments, albeit ones which present important challenges for Spain's young democracy.

Well aware of the capital importance of technological and industrial modernisation, the country's administrative authorities are determinedly following this road, and have introduced various overall arrangements to encourage its pursuit.

As a start, an Act on reconversion and re-industrialisation was adopted in November 1983. This Act was mainly directed to zones and sectors then in decline : it provided various forms of financial assistance, under favourable conditions, to enterprises in process of reconversion, and by similar means encouraged the creation of regional development undertakings.

More recently a Bill enacted in 1986 concerning science and technology, emphasized the country's determination to develop scientific and technical research, and hence expand innovative capacity. (Throughout this report, we will refer to a Bill on Science and Technology as the study was carried out in 1985, i.e. before the Bill was enacted).

It is noteworthy that the OECD experts, in examining Spain's new policies of innovation, have found no major criticism to make of the principal measures envisaged by the Bill concerning science and technology. They noted only a number of gaps, important but not difficult to fill, and there is every reason to suppose that the country is laying a sound foundation for future success.

It is clear that the new Bill on science and technology is the most important step so far taken by Spain towards setting up a policy of innovation. That is why the OECD's examining group, taking due note of this development, has analysed the Bill with great care, and has put forward a number of recommendations to enable the maximum benefit to be derived from it.

Nevertheless it should be emphasized that the promotion of research is only one aspect of a policy designed to encourage innovation. Such a policy must in fact also call for measures to improve the transfer and application of research results to the economy, for better diffusion of new technologies, for the creation of new enterprises, and so on.

Which means that, to be fully effective, administrative action must cover many other aspects besides the promotion of research including industrial research: development of technological services, finance for innovation and the structure of the banking system, professional training, general education, even going so far as the promotion, throughout the population, of a general innovative approach.

There is no doubt that the Spanish Government has adopted such measures in every relevant field. Particularly to be noted is the establishment of a Centre for Technological and Industrial Development (CDTI) set up in 1976 with World Bank assistance to help enterprises – through financial aid and various forms of consultancy – with the introduction of innovation.

The OECD's examining experts also reported that Spain possesses a solid core of scientists and engineers, of very high quality if as yet numerically insufficient. That core must be developed and provided with effective resources for its work.

Despite these positive conclusions, however, the examining experts considered that actions taken which were not directly related to the promotion of research, and more specifically to the encouragement of innovation, were on the whole inadequate. The experts therefore recommended a series of further measures, taking full account both of existing infrastructures and of the new administrative structures now being introduced, particularly in the framework of regionalisation. In this regard it is appropriate to stress the importance of regional structures for modern development, as has been shown in many cases throughout the world.

Summary

Concerning, first of all, further refinement of the Bill covering research and technology, the most important points identified for criticism were as follows:

a) Although the measures envisaged to improve research programming and management seem excellent on the whole, they are essentially administrative in nature. There is therefore a risk of excessive red tape in a country which has demonstrated that enterprising groups can achieve good work spontaneously, even though resources have often been inadequate. The new scientific and technological policies should in fact be under the authority not of a committee, however well selected, but of one very distinguished individual.

b) The attention given to developing and rationalising the infrastructure for carrying out research is probably insufficient. A major effort is required here, and it needs to be mentioned in the text of the Bill.

In particular, within research as a whole there is a need to pinpoint basic research and to define the respective purviews of university research and public institutes for basic research, laying down procedures for them to co-operate with one another.

It would also be desirable to consolidate all applied research laboratories in agriculture under a single authority. (Since the time this recommendation was made, a plan for agronomic R & D has been introduced.) The same applies to certain other applied research sectors, especially public works. More broadly, the research potential of the technological ministries requires strengthening.

c) Since the new status proposed for the five leading research establishments appears to be a notable advance, it is not clear why it should not be extended to all research agencies. (The five research establishments concerned account for 90 per cent of total spending. The remaining 10 per cent are distributed among a rather large number of small research agencies. Applying this new status to those agencies seems likely to raise cost problems.)

d) The budgetary commitment has not been quantified: the Bill would make a far stronger impression on public opinion if it made provision for a regularly increasing percentage of GNP to be allocated for research and for supporting innovation, and if it gave percentage growth targets for the next five years. Of course, present legislative practice may not permit the setting of such expenditure targets.

The experts also stressed the importance of getting the general public to understand why innovation has to be supported. Certain measures have been proposed with this end in view. The broad process of change must be made to encompass the banking system, at present too retail-oriented and insufficiently interested in industrial development: likewise industry whose commitment to research and innovation needs to be considerably stepped up, especially by establishing in-house scientific and technological potential. The new approach should also prompt a rise in the number and resources of venture capital firms.

One point not taken up in the report is that of success criteria for publicly-funded projects. They will certainly be laid down in future by the agencies responsible for scientific and industrial policies. But it must be recalled that such criteria will differ according to whether basic research or applied research is concerned. In the case of applied research the success criterion is the passage to industrialisation and commercialisation within reasonable lead times, of the order of three years.

The experts extended their analysis to aspects distinct from those which the Spanish authorities communicated to them, and which seemed to chiefly correspond to a policy for the development of scientific and technological research. In fact it is necessary to clearly distinguish between innovation policy and scientific research, and to further avoid too exclusive an emphasis on advanced technological innovations. Examples were identified of commercially successful innovations which did not draw upon very sophisticated levels of research and/or scientific knowledge, thereby demonstrating the importance of also promoting this type of innovations.

Moreover, the experts noted that although current emphasis is laid on scientific and technical research, Spain has developed a number of elements of an innovation policy which it would be sound to improve and make better use of (research associations, mutual guarantee companies, venture-capital companies, Institute for Medium and Small Industrial Enterprises, etc.). But they also noted some weaknesses with regard to the adequate integration in other domains of government action, such as youth training policies, of relevant aspects (elements) which are essential for the implementation of an efficient innovation policy.

Lastly the experts noted the advantages and hazards of decentralisation. The hazards will be reduced to the extent that central government and autonomous communities can contrive to work in a complementary and concerted manner. Because this issue is so important, a particularly detailed chapter is devoted to it.

The predominant impression is of Spain's determination to set out resolutely along the road to national creativity, as the most important condition for economic independence which will also allow sensible adoption of foreign technologies. Spain starts on its innovation policy with several advantages, but that policy will need to be steered very accurately and informed by much further reflection, based on a plan for the future which probably still needs developing in greater detail.

Part I

GENERAL REPORT

LIST OF ABBREVIATIONS

ASINEL	Asociacion de Industrias Electricas
	Electrical Enterprises Association
CAICYT	Comision Asesora de Investigacion Cientifica y Técnica
	Advisory Committee for Scientific and Technological Research
CCT	Consell Cientific i Tecnologic
	Council for Science and Technology
CDTI	Centro para el Desarrollo Tecnologico Industrial
	Centre for Technological and Industrial Development
CEDEX	Centro de Estudios y Experimentacion
	Centre for Studies and Experimentation
CEOE	Confederacion Espanola de Organizaciones Empresariales
	Spanish Federation of Industrial Leaders' Associations
CEOTMA	Centro de Estudios de Ordenacion Territorial y Medio Ambiente
	Centre for Studies on Land-use Planning and Environment
CESGAR	Confederacion Espanola de Sociedades de Garantias Reciprocas
	Spanish Confederation of Reciprocal Guaranty Societies
CGCYT	Consejo General de la Ciencia et de la Tecnologia
	Higher Council for Science and Technology
CICYT	Comision Interministerial de la Ciencia et de la Tecnologia
	Interministerial Commission for Science and Technology
CIDA	Centro de Investigaciones de la Armada
	Army Research Centre
CIDEM	Centre d'Informacio i de Desenvolupament d'Empreses
	Centre for Information and Development of Firms
CIRIT	Commissio Interdepartamental de Recerca i Innovacio Tecnologica
	Interdepartmental Commission for Research and Innovation
CSIC	Consejo Superior de Investigaciones Cientificas
	Higher Council for Scientific Research
CTI	Centro Técnico Informatico
	Information Technology Centre
ENISA	Empresa Nacional de Innovacion SA
	National Innovation Company
ESA	European Space Agency
FIS	Fondo de Investigaciones Sanitarias
	Health Research Fund
FUINCA	Fundacion de la Red de Informacion Cientifica Automatizada
	Computerised Scientific Information Network Foundation

ICI	Instituto de Cooperacion Iberoamericana
	Institute for Ibero-american co-operation
IEO	Instituto Espanol de Oceanografia
	Spanish Oceanographic Institute
IGME	Instituto Geologico y Minero de Espana
	Spanish Geological and Mining Institute
IMPI	Instituto de la Mediana y Pequena Empresa Industrial
	Institute for Small and Medium-Sized Industrial Enterprises
INH	Instituto Nacional de Hidrocarburos
	National Hydrocarbon Institute
INI	Instituto Nacional de Industria
	National Industry Institute
INIA	Instituto Nacional de Investigacion Agraria
	National Institute for Agricultural Research
INSALUD	Instituto Nacional de la Salud
	National Health Institute
INTA	Instituto Nacional de Tecnicas Aeroespaciales
	National Aerospace Technology Institute
JEN	Junta de Energia Nuclear
	Nuclear Energy Agency
MAE	Ministerio de Asuntos Exteriores
	Ministry of Foreign Affairs
MAPA	Ministerio de Agricultura, Pesca y Alimentacion
	Ministry of Agriculture, Fisheries and Food
MEC	Ministerio de Educacion y Ciencia
	Ministry for Education and Science
MINER	Ministerio de Industria y Energia
	Ministry for Industry and Energy
MOPU	Ministerio de Obras Publicas y Urbanismo
	Ministry of Public Works and Urban Planning
MTC	Ministerio de Transportes, Turismo y Comunicaciones
	Ministry of Transport, Tourism and Communications
OCIDE	Oficina de Coordinacion de Investigacion y Desarrollo Eléctrico
	Bureau for the Co-ordination of Electrical Research and Development
OPIS	Oficinas Publicas de Investigacion
	State Research Agencies
PEIN	Plan Electronico e Informatico Nacional
	National Plan for Electronics and Informatics
PIU	Programa de Investigacion de las Empresas Eléctricas de UNESA
	Research Programme for UNESA's Electrical Enterprises
SME	Small and Medium-sized Enterprises
SGR	Sociedad de Garantias Reciprocas
	Reciprocal Guarantee Society
SODIS	Sociedades de Desarrollo Industrial
	Industrial Development Societies

SOGASA	Sociedad de Garantias subsidiarias SA Subsidiary Guarantee Company
UNESA	Union Eléctrica SA

I. INTRODUCTION

Technological innovation is an essential factor in any development policy. It is the main precondition for a country's independence, its economic progress and its balanced integration into world trade flows. But unlike discovery and invention, intellectual processes, innovation is essentially a social process. Invention and discovery are admittedly frequently the fruit of certain social and cultural situations, but they do not affect these situations, while innovation sometimes causes very far-reaching changes.

Technological innovation as a *social process* is by nature a complex phenomenon made up of scientific, technical, economic, financial and even psychological components. It is intended to meet a need of society, present or future, a need sometimes not yet felt in the present. It is part of a *systems structure* in which all the elements interact. Hence the difficulty in studying it and the even greater difficulty in trying to stimulate and orient it – in some cases a very minor action will trigger innovation while in others a comprehensive bundle of diverse measures has to be introduced: In most cases it is necessary to determine the points in the chain that constitutes the innovation process at which the effort should be applied. At each of these points there are actors – public or private, legal or physical persons – whose motivations have to be taken into account, and these motivations are by no means always simply financial.

Apart from the case of mere substitution of manufacturing processes – although even here there may be problems of training or retraining the manpower required – technological innovation has social repercussions or even calls for *social innovation*. The inverse is also frequently seen, however – social innovations do not take on their full significance unless accompanied by the technological innovations that they incite or require. The fact is that it is impossible to limit a study of innovation to its technological aspects only. In considering "innovation policy", the word "policy" retains its full original sense of "administration of the City" with a view to improving the life of its inhabitants. What is more, innovation policy should not simply cover the *production of goods*, but also that of *services*.

The complexity of the innovation process and the difficulties encountered when trying to incite, orient and control it makes it worth taking the trouble to analyse the policies implemented in this field in different countries. This exercise is often known as *evaluation*. This designation is perhaps a little pretentious as a policy should be judged on its results, while innovation policies, often very recent, will not bear fruit until some future date. It is more a matter of joint reflection on past and present experience and projects for the future than a judgement, which would be very difficult to formulate. The *transfer of experience* aspect of any evaluation exercise is certainly essential.

The case of Spain is particularly interesting for a joint reflection on innovation policies. Although an industrialised and modern country, Spain, like many others, had not completed its industrial revolution when other causes of evolution appeared – need for new services, development of informatics and robotics, biotechnologies, etc. – so that the country finds itself

17

having to try to complete its industrial development in a context that has not only changed, but is still evolving rapidly.

In addition, Spain may be confronted with a *change in its economic space* with its entry to the Common Market coming at the very moment when the development of *Ibero-Latin-American solidarity* may also constitute an element in its policy.

Lastly, Spain is *culturally* fully developed, with particularly interesting ideas flourishing.

The Spanish innovation policy evaluation exercise is thus particularly difficult, but at the same time particularly interesting and instructive. Although necessarily very limited in time,

Figure 1

SCHEMATIC DIAGRAM OF THE PROCESS OF INNOVATION

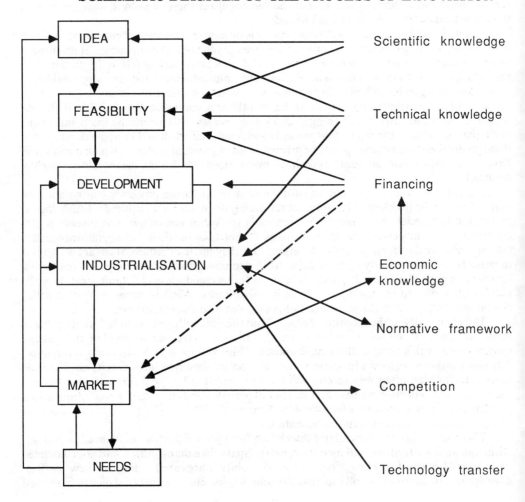

Figure 2

SCHEMATIC DIAGRAM OF THE SPANISH STRUCTURES INVOLVED IN THE INNOVATION PROCESS

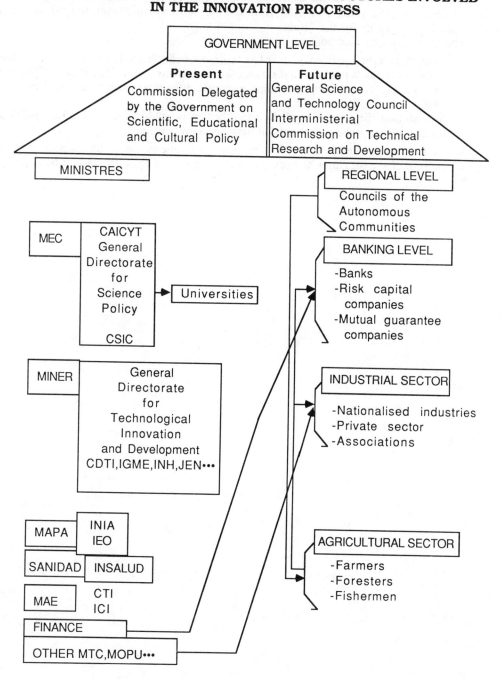

the exercise has to be prepared. This is the aim of this *introductory report*. It could logically have contained three distinct parts, the first being devoted to a general analysis of the possible contents of innovation policies, the second describing the problem of innovation in Spain, and the last discussing the questions arising from the measures already taken to deal with this problem or envisageable for the future.

The Secretariat considered:

- *First*, that the first part would have to a large extent duplicated information contained in *Innovation policy: trends and perspectives* published by the OECD in 1982 on the basis of a meeting of senior officials responsible for innovation policy held in June 1980;
- *Second*, that the separation of the two other parts would have involved a repetition tending to make the document too long and cumbersome.

It was therefore decided to limit this document to a simple exposé of the Spanish problem with an analysis of the measures already taken and mention of those that might be taken in future.

II. TRAINING PEOPLE

Innovation requires actors possessing both particular *aptitudes* and particular *attitudes*. The number, quality and motivation of these actors are the essential factors in the success of innovation; all other factors, however vital they may be, such as the financing possibilities, loose all their effectiveness in the absence of a well-developed human potential.

Giving people the necessary aptitudes is the task of education, which also helps to form attitudes favourable to creativity and the spirit of enterprise. But, education is not the only factor here – the influence of the social environment and its system of values is probably dominant, though it is not possible to precisely determine the most important features. It is known, however, that it is dangerous for the development of new enterprises to give too much emphasis to purely intellectual values at the expense of those connected with action and efficiency.

It is also known that aptitudes develop right throughout a long, never completed, training process in which training in research is a very important stage, while attitudes can be developed and established at a very early age.

It would therefore be interesting to know:

– How are primary and secondary teaching programmes organised to develop aptitudes for scientific and technological research, personal creativity and the spirit of enterprise?
– How does higher education prepare scientists and engineers for their role as researchers/creators/entrepreneurs?
– How does the educational system enable those who have once left it to return to acquire the knowledge that has turned out to be necessary for them to achieve their objectives?

The documents available to the Secretariat in this field provide but imperfect answers to these questions.

In order for an innovation policy to be able to rest on a solid base, primary and secondary education has to:

– Direct a sufficient number of bright students towards science and technology;
– Train students in scientific reasoning while developing their practical sense;
– Give them a taste for technological adventure.

Figures are needed to give a precise assessment of these teaching programmes, particularly by providing an answer to the following questions :

What proportion of pupils emerging from these levels of education are suited for technological and/or scientific training?

Do these levels of education give sufficiently concrete training, thanks in particular to practical work? Is the associated equipment concerned satisfactory?

Do these levels of education devote sufficient time to the history of major technologies and the role of industrial activity?

21

For students completing higher education, figures are available concerning the fields of study (Table 1).

Table 1. **Number of students by discipline**

	Exact and natural sciences	Technology and engineering	Medical sciences	Agricultural sciences	Social sciences	Humanities
1972-73	2 955	2 201	3 355	424	3 270	4 507
1975-76	3 860	3 049	6 444	459	6 706	6 058
1978-79	5 503	2 730	9 726	728	13 162	8 474
1981-82	5 822	2 613	12 722	790	17 047	9 309

Source: Memorandum for the Preparation of a Bill on the Development and Co-ordination of Scientific and Technological Research, 1984.

The overall growth is impressive, total numbers almost tripling in ten years. But the numbers studying the exact sciences only doubled and technology remained about the same while the numbers taking medecine almost quadrupled and the social services increased almost five-fold. The stagnation in technology is so serious that it might be asked whether these figures, taken from a Memorandum for the Preparation of a Bill on the Development and Co-ordination of Scientific and Technological Research (Madrid, 1984) are accurate.

Quantitative data alone do not suffice to define a scientific and technological potential, however, they need to be accompanied by qualitative considerations that are not revealed by statistics.

One indication of this "quality" could be provided by the amount of practical work. For this it would be necessary to have data concerning laboratory expenditure per student in the different disciplines. This figure is often difficult to obtain because it is hidden under other headings. Nevertheless at least a rough order of magnitude should be available.

The training of research workers is a vital element in any policy to develop research and innovation. In some countries, this constitutes the highest "cycle" of the curriculum. The documents available to the Secretariat do not permit to determine:

Whether the preparation for research forms the subject of clearly identifiable teaching in the different universities, and if so, what its relative importance is?

In practice, this training for research is mainly achieved thanks to well-directed thesis preparation. *There are thought to be about 4 500 students preparing theses in Spanish universities. It is essential to know their breakdown by discipline.* It would seem that most doctorate theses are devoted to basic research, even in the engineering schools.

In order to be able to prepare a thesis it is necessary to have financial resources, these usually taking the form of a grant. The grants system in Spain is growing rapidly, the number more than doubling between 1982 and 1984. The total for grants from all sources in 1984 is in the order of Ptas 1 800 million, corresponding to about 2 800 grants. On top of this figure there are grants for study abroad (a little under 300), often resulting from bilateral agreements. It should be pointed out, for example, that on entering the NATO grants system, Spain wisely opted for the solution of reserving all these grants for established researchers of the highest level, until then little concerned by the traditional grants system. The breakdown of these grants by discipline is important and needs to be known. Similarly, it would be useful to know the number of grants awarded in relation to the number of candidates.

In order to maintain a high level of research in both industry and the universities, it is necessary for the knowledge of those involved in research to be constantly updated. Spain has launched a training programme for academics involving stays in foreign laboratories, particularly in the United States. This programme is only in its infancy, but holds promise.

Another method consists of allowing a certain mobility for university staff, who can work in other laboratories public or private, national or foreign, from time to time. This is partly the role of further training grants, but it is also, and above all, *the role of the sabbatical year, which does not appear very widespread in Spain.*

The above concerns teaching staff. Taking the case of research workers themselves, whether in the public or private sector, the question is whether they have access to all the opportunities for further training, documentation, seminars, special courses, etc., that they need. This question will not be asked formally here, but its implications will be seen in most of the questions posed below. Its importance must never be forgotten.

All the above is concerned with the problem of training the human scientific and technical research potential, the prime concern of any policy to promote innovation. It seems certain that this problem is felt to be important by the Spanish Authorities and considerable progress has already been made, but there still remains an enormous amount to do, as shown by the data analysed at the end of this Chapter.

The total number of scientists and engineers working on research and development in 1985 amounted to only 18 000 approximately, in full-time equivalent (for 40 000 to 50 000 researchers involved). The universities and the CSIC (defined in the next Chapter) account for three quarters of them, hence the great, and certainly excessive, predominance of the Ministry for Education and Science in scientific and technological policy matters.

The private sector accounts for only one fifteenth of this potential. As for the sectoral research bodies, the numbers employed in R&D are in general not enough to reach the critical mass, the average age is often high (about 45) and competences are often badly distributed (an inadequate number of engineers even in the Junta de Energia Nuclear – Nuclear Energy Commission: one sixth).

By and large, the human resources devoted to engineering and technology, i.e. transforming knowledge into products and services, are inadequate.

In addition, the geographical distribution of these resources is very uneven. Heavy concentration in Madrid and Catalonia (37.5 and 21.3 per cent respectively); much lower

Table 2. **Number of researchers and graduates for certain countries**

Country	Year	Graduates per 10 000 inhabitants A	Researchers per 100 000 inhabitants B	Ratio B/A
Spain	1979	101	26	0.257
Argentina	1980	196	35	0.179
Portugal[1]	1978	111	21	0.189
Venezuela[1]	1980	64	31	0.484
Italy	1978	98	71	0.725
France	1979	233	136	0.584
Canada	1979	256	108	0.422
Germany	1979	322	198	0.615
Japan	1980	353	367	1.040
United States[2]	1980	118	277	2.348

1. Estimates.
2. Figures for the United States are probably not comparable.
Source: Propuesta del Programa de Ciencia y Tecnologia para el Desarrollo V Centenario, Cyted-D, 1983.

numbers, but still well above the rest of the country, in Andalusia and the Community of Valencia (11.2 and 6.8 per cent), so that four regions account for three quarters of the total. This is a serious situation at a time when Spain is trying to implement a balanced regional policy.

The figures contained in Table 2, though approximate, allow comparison with other countries.

Spain has clearly made great progress since 1980, but the ratio B/A (see Table 2) remains relatively low, which means that graduates are in general not motivated towards research. This reflects the inadequate dynamism of scientific policy in the past, but the situation can be rectified very quickly once an appropriate policy is resolutely pursued.

III. THE DEVELOPMENT OF SCIENTIFIC KNOWLEDGE

Most technologies today are developed on the basis of scientific knowledge. It is therefore normal that those responsible for a policy to encourage innovation in a country should consider the quality of basic research, the results of which can form the foundation for technological progress. The Memorandum for the Preparation of a Bill on the Development and Co-ordination of Scientific and Technological Research, therefore devotes considerable space to analysing research system in Spain.

For convenience, this Chapter will deal only with fundamental (or basic) research, aimed above all at contributing to knowledge, while the following Chapter will be devoted to applied research. It must be stressed, however, that the distinction is not rigid and the two types of research have many points in common and are often carried out in the same institutions and directed by the same bodies.

However, in the case of Spain it would appear that the desirable interaction between these two types of research has not yet come about and that present efforts are directed precisely at establishing the necessary inter-connections where they do not yet exist.

For sake of clarity it is convenient to split the functions of scientific and technological institutions into four "levels":

- Level 1: planning, development and co-ordination;
- Level 2: science programming and administration;
- Level 3: carrying out of research and exploitation of results;
- Level 4: auxiliary services (often integrated with the other levels).

The Memorandum mentioned above considers that the difficulty encountered in Spain in establishing a true scientific and technological policy and defining priorities is due to:

- The superposition of institutions whose functions more or less overlap;
- The extreme dispersion of research between the various ministries and public research bodies (the OPIS).

Thus, at level 1, there are:

- The Interministerial Commission on Educational, Cultural and Scientific Policy, delegated by the government ("Delegated Commission");
- The Advisory Commission for Scientific and Technological Research, CAICYT (Comision Asesora de Investigacion Cientifica y Técnica) which comes under the Ministry for Education and Science;
- The Higher Council for Scientific Research, CSIC (Consejo Superior de Investigaciones Cientificas), which comes under the same Ministry;
- The General Directorate for Scientific Policy, one of the departments of the same Ministry;
- The General Directorate for Industrial Innovation and Technology, one of the departments of the Ministry for Industry and Energy;

- The Centre for Technological and Industrial Development, CDTI, also coming under the Ministry for Industry and Energy.

At level 2 there are:

- CAICYT (Ministry for Education and Research);
- CDTI (Ministry for Industry and Energy);
- FIS (Fondo de investigaciones sanitarias) or Health Research Fund, coming under the Ministry for Health and Consumer Affairs.

At level 3 there are:

a) For basic research and coming under the Ministry for Education and Research:
  - CSIC;
  - The universities.

b) for sectoral research, mainly applied, but sometimes including some basic research:
  - In addition to the CSIC, which is a multisectoral research body, over a dozen institutes coming under various ministries;
  - Laboratories attached to public enterprises and services;
  - Laboratories of private enterprises;
  - Associations and foundations;
  - Regional centres (of the Autonomous Communities).

These bodies will be listed in the following Chapter because of their distinctly "applied" character.

The above shows the multiplicity of authorities for a single mission and the multiplicity of missions for a single authority.

The Delegated Commission seems to have been able neither to programme nor to co-ordinate, probably because the field to be covered was too broad (education, culture and science), but also because other bodies had already taken charge of at least part of its role.

CAICYT[1], set up in 1958, modified its type of activity in 1963 when the Delegated Commission was instituted and tried to become the tool of this Commission by serving as a link with the network of pure and applied research centres. For this purpose CAICYT disposes of the National Fund for the Development of Scientific Research, established in 1964 and funded as follows (in millions of pesetas):

Years	1968/69	1970/71	1972	1973	1974	1975
Million Ptas	100	250	175	632	875	1 113

From 1976 to 1981 the figure remained about the same as in 1975, then there was a big jump in 1982 to about Ptas 7 500 million. The figure for 1983 was Ptas 7 009.7 million. This quantitative change obviously also brought about a qualitative change.

At first the financing of "projects" came to be added to the financing of freely chosen research topics, then came to replace them, forming the beginnings, fairly timid, of a "policy" in 1979. Before this date most of the research projects resulted from very open invitations to apply for funding. Without going into great detail, it can be said that CAICYT developed an effective mechanism for evaluating and selecting projects during this period, this being based on internal analysis and the advice of expert committees. At present CAICYT is responsible for:

- Selecting worthwhile projects capable of advancing knowledge and hence supporting the "policy of pure scientists";
- Promoting research useful for future economic development according to priorities established at the level of the Delegated Commission.

CAICYT can take action with any research centre, basic or applied, public or private. The procedures used vis-à-vis industrial laboratories will be discussed in the next chapter.

CSIC is an independent body, a legal entity with its own resources, placed under the authority of the Ministry for Education and Science. It accounts for 25 per cent of State financed research and it is thus a vital tool in Spanish research policy.

At first, it seems to have operated virtually independently and set up a network of its own laboratories and co-ordinated outside laboratories covering all scientific fields. This network which included 88 laboratories at the beginning of 1985 is obviously difficult to manage and there has been criticism of the lack of communication between management and laboratories and between the laboratories themselves. (The number of laboratories was reduced down to 81 during the year 1985.)

Since 1981, however, CSIC has made an effort to organise its activities not simply according to scientific discipline, but increasingly by means of targeted programmes – biomedecine and health, energy, agrobiology and food, biotechnologies, industrial products and new technologies, human and social sciences.

In addition, it establishes scientific agreements with public or private bodies, Spanish or foreign.

It should be recalled that CSIC plays an important part in training researchers through the 1 000 grants that it awards to enable scientists to work in its own laboratories and in other institutions.

Lastly, CSIC is very active with regard to publications – books, monographs, specialist journals.

The importance of this body justifies to detail the breakdown of its budget and staff by field of activities (for 1983).

Of this total budget, it appears that only 17.6 per cent (or Ptas 2 479 million) is used directly to finance research projects associated with a policy which intends to be realistic and adapted to circumstances. Tables 3 and 4 lack detail, but do raise a number of questions, that will be formulated below.

CSIC employs about 5 000 people (2 000 of whom are scientific personnel payed by CSIC on permanent agents of this organism) and staff costs amount to 69.7 per cent of total expenditure. Equipment accounts for 6.3 per cent, investment 11.5 per cent and administration for 6.9 per cent. The figure of Ptas 1.5 million per researcher per year to carry out his work should therefore be viewed with extreme caution – it is probable that the real figure is in fact lower and in any case lower than is usual in other countries.

All these data lead to the following conclusions:

i) CSIC is an important body, but tends to scatter its efforts, hence a risk of inefficiency, with many of its units probably not reaching the critical mass;

ii) The share of applied research, to which we shall return in the following Chapter, is certainly very considerable at least 33 per cent. It should be noted that 18 per cent of the budget comes from parafiscal taxes on a number of industries including steel and cement, etc.;

iii) It is therefore difficult to determine the influence of CSIC in the field of basic research and the policy pursued by it in this field.

Table 3. **The budget of CSIC**

Million Ptas

Scientific fields	Personnel + ordinary budget + investments		National fund (CAICYT)		Contracted research		Total		Percent	
	1983	1985	1983	1985	1983	1985	1983	1985	1983	1985
Human and social sciences	899	1 015	98	44	3	13	1 000	1 072	7.0	6.3
Biology, biomedicine	1 449	1 664	275	140	53	101	1 777	1 905	12.6	11.1
Agronomy	1 982	2 230	128	92	32	166	2 142	2 518	15.2	14.6
Natural resources	1 606	1 580	128	98	103	294	1 837	1 972	13.1	11.5
Physics and physics technology	1 045	1 225	120	318	21	229	1 186	1 772	8.4	10.3
Chemistry and chemical technology	1 273	1 494	163	139	20	160	1 456	1 793	10.3	10.4
Food science and technology	1 036	1 184	85	80	37	72	1 158	1 336	8.2	7.8
Materials technology	1 566	1 885	57	34	67	392	1 690	2 311	12.0	13.5
General scientific services	550	655	9	57	63	71	622	783	4.4	4.6
Administrative services	1 196	1 564	–	72	–	67	1 196	1 703	8.5	9.9
Total	12 602	14 526	1 063	1 074	399	1 565	14 064	17 165	100.0	100.0

Source : CSIC, May 1985, February 1987.

Table 4. **Expenditures of the CSIC**

	Million Ptas		Percentage	
	1983	1985	1983	1985
Staff	9 810	10 913	69.7	63.6
Training of research staff	296	355	2.1	2.0
Current expenditures *of which:*				
Administration	965	1 058	6.9	6.2
Fungible material and magazines	890	1 265	6.3	7.4
Travel and *per diem*	216	394	1.5	2.3
Publications	195	184	1.4	1.1
Subsidies	73	129	0.5	0.7
Investment *of which:*				
Stock items and equipment	1 178	2 065	8.4	12.0
Buildings	441	802	3.1	4.7
Total	14 064	17 165	100.0	100.0

Source: CSIC, May 1985, February 1987.

University research

The aims of university research are:

- To ensure the competence of the teacher in his field;
- Provide him with the means for improving knowledge in his field.

This boils down to saying that as from a certain level, teaching is inseparable from research and this research is essentially oriented by the logic of contributing to knowledge.

Thus, teacher-researchers in all countries claim complete freedom for search and do not want it to be directed towards short-term applications.

This does not imply, however, that the teacher necessarily has to carry out research in his own laboratory – he can do it anywhere provided that his liberty is respected.

It does not imply either that he should not participate in targeted research programmes, oriented to satisfy needs, in which his competence can be of great help. In universities one expects to find a certain amount of applied research which may or may not be carried out on a contract basis. Such research may also have a beneficial effect on university research proper by helping to pinpoint gaps in knowledge which need to be filled.

If scientific, technological and innovation policy is intended to have an impact on university research – and that is its job – it must be understood that action should be directed not at the research itself, but further upstream, on the relative importance to be accorded to each discipline or to each multidisciplinary topic and on orientation towards those fields considered particularly important both from the standpoint of contributing to knowledge and that of the possible socio-economic spinoff.

It should also be noted that the step from pure to applied knowledge is sometimes very short (theory of polymerisation and the production of plastics, for example), but may also sometimes be extremely long (as in certain branches of mathematics or theoretical physics).

It should also be noted that the contents of certain courses are by the nature of things very close to applications (in the engineering sciences, for example).

Summarising, universities must have the means:

– To freely develop their own research;
– To participate to the full extent of their competence in the national research policy.

Do Spanish universities have the resources to carry out their own research? The breakdown of university research expenditure in 1983 was as follows:

Table 5. **Budget for university research**

Million Ptas

Research share of university staff costs	10 300
Grants for research students	1 600
Sub-total	11 900
Research share of university operating expenditure	806
Share of university investment	307
Sundry	725
Sub-total	1 838
Transfers from the National Fund	3 055
Transfers from other ministries	261
Transfers from the private sector	442
Funds stemming from international co-operation	105
Total	17 601

Source: See Table 1.

Thus apart from the personnel costs, only one third of the sums devoted to research come from the universities' budget. This would not be too serious if these sums were substantial, but they are not. If they are divided by the number of university teachers (about 24 000)[2] they only amount to:

- Ptas 76 000 from the university
- Ptas 161 000 from other sources

making a total of Ptas 237 000.

Even taking account of the fact that not all university teachers are researchers, but including research students, the figure is still very modest – in the order of Ptas 500 000 (while the very optimistic figure of Ptas 1.7 million appears in certain documents). The corresponding figures for other research bodies are very much higher – Ptas 5.2 million for agricultural research, 6.9 million for the National Hydrocarbon Institute, 8.2 million for the CSIC and 10.6 million for nuclear energy.

In broad terms, the universities research has only one-tenth of a per capita sum which already appears barely adequate in other institutions. On top of this there is a further aggravating factor – the universities do not seem to have the technical staff necessary for the proper carrying out of research.

This is a serious situation. The university potential is considerably under-utilised and the bodies that in theory should allocate funds in accordance with a comprehensive scientific policy, such as CAICYT, are obliged to simply act as lifebuoys so that university research can survive.

Even in a field where universities play an important role, even if only because of the number of students – medical sciences – the Health Research Fund of the Ministry for Health (FIS) provided only Ptas 194 million in 1983 (44 million of which in the form of grants).

It is essential to realise that no policy aimed at scientific development and innovation can base itself on university research so long as the latter has not reached the critical threshold, which means multiplying the sums devoted to research activities, excluding personnel costs, by at least five.

In fact, in order to maintain the level of dependency of universities on external resources below 50 per cent so as to keep this research sector fully free and dynamic, university funds devoted to research should be increased by a factor of 15. This should be seen as a fairly short-term objective. The universities will then be in a position to provide their country with the essential knowledge base, and to improve this base. They will then be able to play the major role that they should have in a national innovation policy, thanks to research contracts. The quality of Spanish university teachers and students merits this national effort.

IV. THE DEVELOPMENT OF TECHNICAL KNOWLEDGE

The development of technological knowledge takes place – or ought to take place – in two different environments, one where technology is taught, mainly in universities and engineer training schools, and the other where it is used, mainly industry, industrial associations and certain high technology centres devoted, for example, to nuclear energy or space.

It is essential to have as close a link as possible between those responsible for technological research and the industries likely to exploit its findings, whether these involve simply technical progress or true innovation. It is by no means certain that this link is as strong as it should be in Spain, a country that is marked by a number of paradoxical situations, not found in other European countries, that will be examined in this Chapter.

Universities rightly consider basic research to be an end in itself, but this is not a reason for them to keep away from research oriented towards short or medium-term economic progress, at the appropriate level. The fact is that the universities receive money for carrying out research that very definitely falls in the applied category. A closer analysis of Table 5 is necessary here, however. Of the sums transferred to the universities from the National Fund, Ptas 1 360 million come under the heading of "research projects" and 80 under "concerted plans". We shall return to these latter below. *As concerns the projects, it would be useful to know the proportions of those concerned with basic research and those concerned with targeted research, i.e. oriented towards applications.*

The funds provided by ministries other than education can be considered as destined for targeted research aimed at specific applications. The Ptas 261 million appearing under this heading are broken down as follows:

- 194: Ministry of Health (via FIS);
- 36: Ministry for Industry and Energy (via the Centre for Energy Studies);
- 3: Same Ministry but via the CTDI (see below);
- 27: Ministry of Agriculture.

With the exception of the Ptas 194 million from the FIS which underlines the vigorous development of medical sciences in the universities (in this case pure and applied research are closely linked) it can be seen that the sums involved are very small, not to say ridiculous. In the case of the technical ministries the universities seem to play only a marginal role.

The funds from the private sector, though not enormous – Ptas 442 million – are high enough to give the impression that the universities do have some fairly significant industrial contracts. This is not the case, however, as is shown by Table 6 which gives the breakdown of this Ptas 442 million.

Thus only half of this total can be considered as going to fund applied technological research. It may be, however, that there is a more or less underground system of direct contracts between enterprises and university teachers. It is probably fairly small and does not appear in the statistics.

Table 6. **Funds from the private sector**

Million Ptas

Foundations	:	Barrié de la Maza	130.86
		University & enterprise	4.50
		Against cancer	18.74
		Ramon Areces	60.00
Enterprises	:	MAPFRE	3.60
		CECA	203.23
Associations	:	Anthropos	3.00
		Northwest metallurgy research	0.67
		ASINEL (see below)	0.32
		Shipping research	0.45
		Transport research	10.00
Post-graduate Technological Institute			7.00
Total			442.37

Source: See Table 1.

It is in fact the system of research contracts between industry and university laboratories that provides the best way for the universities to exploit their knowledge in the industrial environment, and in turn receive useful information from it, and for industry to raise its level of research and fill any gaps in a particular field that appear to be important at a given moment.

Although coming under the Ministry for Education and Science, CAICYT has always considered that its function was to finance both pure and applied research. Paradoxically, it was CAICYT that created the research associations for the developement of collective research in enterprises in 1961, and not the Ministry for Industry and Energy. CAICYT also set up two original mechanisms for financing research and innovation in 1968:

a) "Concerted research plans" with aid to research in enterprises in the form of no-interest loans covering 50 per cent of the research budget;

b) "Co-ordinated concerted plans" aiding projects carried on jointly by an enterprise and one or more public research bodies. Aid can cover 100 per cent of the project budget (and it even appears that at least part of this aid can be in the form of subsidy).

Between 1968 and the end of 1982, 469 projects had been assisted in this way (out of 1 437 applications), for a total budget of Ptas 18 500 million, 46 per cent through loans by the Administration. The breakdown of these concerted plans is given in Table 7 below.

The Table shows that the accent is on heavy technologies. It should be noted that the applications are examined by CAICYT but have to be approved by the Delegated Commission. In addition to financing, CAICYT monitors projects and acts as advisor.

As from 1984 CAICYT has shown some other interesting initiatives. First, the new call for applications for co-ordinated concerted plans was made on 30th March 1984 in close liaison with CDTI, a body to be described below, which comes under the Ministry for Industry and Energy. Second, grouped activities that might be called "major programmes" have developed, though certain of them are still in the evaluation or planning stage. CAICYT is organising itself for assessing such projects by setting up fairly broadly based committees.

Table 7.

Table 7. **Concerted plans up to 1983**

Field	Number	%	Budget	Loans	%
			Million Ptas		
Agriculture and Food	53	11	1 280	541	6
Pharmacy	56	12	1 584	664	8
Engineering[1]	126	27	6 034	2 834	33
Electrical and Electronics	125	27	5 649	2 641	31
Chemicals & parachemicals	109	23	4 136	1 853	22
Total	469	100	18 683	8 533	100

1. This includes various technologies not included under other headings.
Source: Ministry of Industry, Madrid.

Its *de facto* interministerial role is now obvious. The major programmes are:

Agro-energy: biomass in the form of either cultivated energy crops or waste products. This research is in liaison with the universities, the Nuclear Energy Commission, the National Agronomic Research Institute, etc.

Aquaculture: programme started by a reporting committee (ponencia) chaired by the Director General for the Organisation (ordenacion) of Fisheries, covering:
- 5 projects and 16 concerted plans;
- The creation of an aquaculture documentation centre in collaboration with CSIC and INIA;
- A training plan.

Micro-electronics: programme including activities ranging from concerted plans to training projects and concerning the Ministry for Industry, the Ministry of Defence, the CSIC and Madrid Polytechnical University. There is also a specific project for the creation of a micro-electronics research and development centre[3].

Improvement of rail transport, a programme that does not yet appear to have taken shape.

CAICYT has also studied two "mobilisation programmes" in the biotechnology and high energy fields.

The dynamic activity of CAICYT has no limits, however. It includes inviting high level foreign academics or engineers to Spain for their sabbatical year, and another aspect of CAICYT activities, research associations, will be discussed below.

CSIC, already discussed, comes under the Ministry for Education. Although it plays an important part in basic research, its activity has extended to technical research right from the beginning. CSIC has an important advantage in this respect – its intersectoral and multidisciplinary nature. While it is open to criticism, it has to be recognised that CSIC is very ready to take responsibility for applied research projects which for the most part call upon several fields of knowledge.

The share of the CSIC budget allocated to the execution of projects in 1983 (16 per cent or 2 479 million pesetas) is funded to the extent of 43 per cent (1 063 million pesetas) by CAICYT, 16 per cent (399 million pesetas) by research contracts, 18 per cent (450 million pesetas) by parafiscal taxes (from the cement, coal and steel industries) and 23 per cent (567 million pesetas) directly by the Ministry for Education.

Although contracts form a small proportion of the total (16 per cent of 16 per cent, it would appear), the CSIC can play the role of a big centre for contract research. It is a supplier of technical research, though demand from enterprises is still weak.

Just as the CSIC had to invent its own policy and establish its own priorities when the promotion of research was not a major concern of the government, it has also had to develop its own contract procedures. In fact, it uses a very flexible system, virtually tailor-made for each individual case:

- Projects subsidised by an enterprise with no return other than the communication of results;
- Projects totally or partly funded by an enterprise with an undertaking by the CSIC not to divulge patentable findings to another enterprise;
- Projects for which the enterprise has full intellectual property rights over the findings, etc.

The CSIC certainly makes a considerable effort to meet demand – often unformulated – of the economic sector and to harmonize its own policies with that being established by the government. The situation is thus evolving. The following questions nevertheless suggest themselves:

- *What is the nature of the links that certainly exist between the CSIC and the Ministry for Industry?*
- *How are the parafiscal taxes used? Does the industry concerned have control over the way they are used?*

In a noteworthy article in the April 1983 edition of *Economia Industrial*, the Vice-Chairman of the CSIC stated that the transfer of the results of research carried out by the CSIC (as in the universities or other research bodies) to industry is made difficult by the CSIC's lack of means for developing innovations and by the imbalance between research supply and demand. In addition, it appears that the majority of small and even medium enterprises are simply not aware of the existence of this very useful infrastructure, the CSIC. This clearly raises the problem of the use and exploitation of research findings.

The CDTI (Centre for Industrial Technological Development) was set up in 1977 as a result of a credit of US $18 million offered by the World Bank for five years (and extended to 31st December 1983). Its aim is to promote the generation of innovative technologies, procedures and products in Spain and its action ranges from technological development to marketing. It thus meets the need pointed out at the end of the previous paragraph with no restrictions on field of activity or geographical region. Its budget has increased as follows:

Year	1979	1980	1981	1982	1983
Budget (million Ptas)	779	1 213	1 339	1 500	1 900

At first an autonomous body of an administrative nature coming under the Ministry for Industry and Energy, CDTI's status was changed by the decree of 30th November 1983 which made it one of the basic instruments for the management of this Ministry's technological policy.

It was in fact limited to one single type of financing: risk participation with costs being spread. Loans, subsidies and capital shares, which in many cases would have been better suited, were excluded. The fact that recovery of the funds contributed is on the basis of a percentage of the sales of products seems to have prevented the CDTI from assisting in the development of processes. 75 per cent of the projects submitted to the CDTI are concerned with product innovation, only 3 per cent coming from the service sector. It should be noted that 70 per cent of various projects were submitted by enterprises employing less than 200 people, a fact which seems to have been criticised but which in fact would appear very

34

positive. It also appears that large firms have not so much wanted to share the risk as to reduce it by an amount known in advance and they have not accepted the additional complex accounting made necessary by meticulous regulations.

But another vital question remains: are the experimental resources at the level of the development of industrial processes adequate in Spain, and if not, who would decide on their creation? This question will not be formulated here, as three types of technical potential can be envisaged at this level of development:

- That of enterprises;
- That of specialised technical centres;
- That of research associations.

The next three paragraphs will provide at least a partial answer to this basic question.

The specialised research centres, although fairly numerous in Spain, do not seem to cover all the fields that they should and in many cases have perhaps not reached the desirable size. The most important ones appear in Table 8, under the appropriate ministry. In addition, research is carried out by the CSIC in such fields as agriculture, oceanography, biomedecine, etc.

Table 8. **Principal specialised research centres**

	Expenditure Million Ptas A	Staff numbers B	A/B
MAPA (Ministry of Agriculture, Fisheries and Food)			
Instituto Nacional de Investigacion Agraria (INIA)	4 471	848	5.2
Instituto Espanol de Oceanografia (IEO)	924	128	7.2
Defence			
Instituto Nacional de Tecnicas de Aeroespaciales (INTA)	5 630	1 510	3.7
Canal	490	119	4.1
CIDA and other centres	–	1 038	–
MINER (Ministry of Industry and Energy)			
Instituto Geologico y Minero de Espana (IGME)	877	97	9.0
Instituto Nacional de Hidrocarburos (INH)	1 963	282	6.9
Junta de Energia Nuclear (JEN)	3 606	339	10.6
MOPU (Ministry of Public Works and Urban Planning)			
Centro de Ordenacion del Territorio y de Medio Ambiente (CEOTMA)	366	40	9.1
Centro de Estudios y Experimentacion (CEDEX)	4 629	398	11.6
M. Sanidad y Consumo (Ministry of Health)			
Instituto Nacional de la Salud (INSALUD)	2 112	515	4.1

Source: See Table 1, and Ministry of Defence.

The figures presented in Table 8 are simply taken from the replies to questionnaires and need to be checked, but their order of magnitude seems plausible. In many cases they show the weaknesses of the system. For example, it is obvious that the Ministry of Defence with 122 people engaged on research cannot play the same role of locomotive for innovation as in many other industrial countries. Similarly, it is doubtful whether CEDEX, which covers in particular the Road Research Laboratory, the Materials Testing Laboratory, the Hydrographic Studies Laboratory and Ports and Coasts has reached such a size as to permit true innovation.

What is more, the figure for expenditure per researcher indicates that many of these bodies are much closer to pure research than to research and development.

It also seems that this system *lacks a national test laboratory, in the broad sense, such as the NBS in the United States or LNE in France, essential for keeping control over standards.*

In addition, the tools that appear essential in order to transform laboratory results into industrial processes that Spain intends to create may be too dispersed, and one may question whether existing centres really have the resources to carry innovation as far as the stage of industrialisation.

Obviously the gaps that can be seen at this level can be compensated by the research effort within enterprises or their research associations.

Research within enterprises is always difficult to evaluate, especially in Spain where there are few statistics on the subject. The figures in Table 9 nevertheless appear plausible.

Table 9. **Research expenditure by sector – 1983**

Sector	Research expenditures Million Ptas	Percent	Percent of GDP[1]
Public administration	68 814	61.5	0.3
Public enterprises	21 429	19.2	0.094
Private enterprises	21 571	19.3	0.095
Total	111 813	100.0	0.489

1. GDP = gross domestic product.
Source: See Table 1.

The participation of enterprises in the national research effort is thus less than the EEC average, though the difference is not great. It should be noted that the public contribution to the research effort of enterprises is only 2.2 per cent as against an EEC average of 14.1 per cent.

There is also the question of the nature of research carried out by enterprises, which may range from routine assistance with the manufacturing process to truly innovative action.

The fact is that a high proportion of Spanish industry is comprised of firms working under foreign licence or subsidiaries of foreign firms. Thus 55 per cent of the capital goods produced in Spain are manufactured under licence. Similarly, 85 per cent of Spanish patents are taken out by foreigners, as against an EEC average of 45 per cent. Considerable quantitative and qualitative differences between sectors are therefore found as shown in Table 10.

These figures are eloquent. Not only is research expenditure low – and in some industries such as construction, agriculture, textiles, etc., a negligible percentage of GDP – but it is also often less than expenditure on technology transfer payments, even in key sectors of the economy. A simple comparison of the totals of technology transfer payments and research expenditure, 0.34 and 0.25 per cent of GDP respectively, shows the risks Spain is running for its future development. The assimilation of imported technologies is a good way to achieve industrial development (as demonstrated by Japan) but on condition that expenditure on the mastery and domestic development of imported technologies and on domestic innovation is

Table 10. **Average annual payments for technology transfer and R&D by sector – 1978-80**

Sector	TTP/GDP[1]	R&D/GDP	A[2]	B[2]
Agriculture	0.03	0.04	0.80	1.45
Extractive industries and oil refining	0.28	0.71	1.44	4.95
Electricity, gas & water	0.94	0.03	6.63	2.82
Steel and non-ferrous metals	0.77	1.15	3.49	6.99
Non-metallic mineral products	0.20	0.59	0.94	3.71
Chemicals	2.43	2.54	15.92	22.54
Metal products and engineering	1.88	1.17	17.56	6.55
Electrical and electronics			11.73	18.18
Transport equipment	2.80	0.85	28.41	11.70
Food, drink and tobacco	0.27	0.21	2.26	2.43
Textiles, leather, clothing	0.25	0.07	2.90	1.12
Paper and printing	0.20	0.14	0.95	0.92
Other manufactures	0.29	0.63	2.78	8.21
Construction	0.11	0.01	2.66	0.38
Services	0.01	0.04	1.53	8.05
Total	0.34	0.25	100.00	100.00

1. TTP = technology transfer payments; GDP = gross national product.
2. A = TTP of the sector as a percentage of the total; B = R&D of the sector as a percentage of the total; A and B show the sectors where an effort is needed.
Source: Ministry of Industry, Madrid.

very much higher (Japan once again) than the technology transfer payment. This point will be taken up again in the following Chapter.

Research associations, or more generally *co-operative research* systems are a good way to:

- Avoid excessive expenditure and duplication of work by pooling the research effort in the non-competitive fields of an industry, these being numerous: measuring and testing techniques, extension of basic university research, evaluation of processes, etc.;
- Enable small enterprises to take part in research by spending reasonable sums while at the same time helping this research to reach the critical mass required for it to be efficient.

Research associations were set up in Spain mainly on the initiative of the CAICYT, which grants subsidies in the order of Ptas 6 million a year on average. There were 24 such associations in 1982.

Most of them were set up simply for prestige reasons and did not start to really try to fulfil their role until the second half of the seventies. This role is vital, not only in research – which is a weak point in virtually all industries – but also through the analysis of the overall problems of a sector, market research, the orientation of development, the spread of information and the further training made necessary by technological progress. There is every advantage to be derived from developing these tools, but unfortunately there are no statistics available to give an idea of the vitality.

What are the budgets of these different associations and what is the relative importance of R&D activities proper, advisory activities, training, etc.? Which of them have their own research facilities? Where these do not exist to whom do they turn for research of general interest to the industry?

In far too many cases these questions remain unanswered.

Judgement on the overall effectiveness of these associations is in general fairly severe, but they could constitute a vital tool for innovation policy.

By way of example let us analyse the case of the electricity industry research association.

This case is exemplary and warrants attention because of its complexity. Electricity generation and distribution and the manufacture of the associated equipment is handled mainly by the private sector and is spread among a great number of firms, many of which are not of sufficient size for efficient research. There is also a public electricity generation and distribution undertaking, UNESA, which belongs to the INI Group.

The private enterprises and some public ones are grouped together in an association, ASINEL, whose aim is to carry out research on a co-operative basis for members. In 1980, ASINEL received Ptas 110 million in subscriptions and 93 million in payment for documentation and research work. The fact is that ASINEL, created in 1965, has a long research history and constitutes a focal point for international co-operation, for example with Mexico. ASINEL is present in all the international bodies of the sector. Its organisation, with seven commissions and 36 specialist committees, enables it to carry out its role to the full. The link with the public sector is through the PIU (programa de investigacion de las empresas electricas de UNESA), a research programme in which ASINEL directs, co-ordinates or monitors a great number of projects for which it sometimes builds laboratories on its own land, such as:

- Medium voltage power test laboratory;
- Low voltage laboratory;
- High voltage dielectric test laboratory;
- High voltage power test laboratory.

All this obviously leads to ASINEL playing a vital role in standardization.

The research programme, as described in the activity report for 1983, appears very complete. Not only does it adequately cover the demands of enterprises, but it includes numerous activities concerned with new energies: 20 MW solar station, photovoltaic panels, hydrocarbon producing plants, wind power – as well as very original ideas such as using fly ash in agriculture.

Summarising, Spain seems to possess a tool perfectly adapted to research and technical innovation in the field of electricity and energy in general. The structure of ASINEL is such as to allow easy transition to the exploitation of findings through member undertakings.

It is nevertheless difficult, because of the close interweaving of public and private undertakings in the electricity industry, to determine the extent to which ASINEL meets the respective needs of the nationalised and private industries.

V. TECHNOLOGY TRANSFERS

No country, however great, can avoid resorting to foreign technologies, and the balance of licence payments alone is not a good indicator of the degree of economic dependence. Table 11 allows cross-country comparisons. Although the data are from 1978, orders of magnitude have probably not changed greatly. The GDP figures are for 1979.

This Table shows that Spain is an atypical case. The amount for licence payments is very low. It is not this that indicates Spain's technological dependence, but another figure, that for technical assistance and services, which amounts to 0.198 per cent of GDP. The total for licence payments plus technical assistance and services thus amounted to 0.280 in 1978 and has grown regularly since (0.423 in 1982) while the share of licence payments in this total is tending to fall (0.067 in 1982).

These figures indicate the importance of the multinationals established in Spain, these enterprises generally making extensive use of assistance contracts. To compensate for this there would have to be Spanish multinationals, but this is not the case.

The ratio of licence receipts to payments should be noted. It is the lowest in Europe.

The comments so far could give the idea that the Spanish situation is like that of Japan, but Table 11 clearly shows the vital difference already mentioned above – Japan makes a far greater research effort in its enterprises.

To have a complete picture of the situation we would have to know the restrictive clauses, and in particular any bans on exporting to certain countries, which accompany the granting of licences to Spanish industry.

Table 11. **Technology payments and receipts, and R&D – 1978**

Percent

Country	Licence payments/GDP	Licence receipts/GDP	(R&D)/GDP for enterprise sector	Receipts/Payments (licences)	GDP per capita (dollars)
United States	0.028	0.257	1.58	894.4	10.563
Sweden	0.156	0.080	1.32	51.1	9.829
Switzerland	0.834	3.247	1.84	389.2	9.707
Germany	0.150	0.067	1.45	44.6	8.500
France	0.114	0.055	1.05	48.2	8.234
Netherlands	0.340	0.211	1.01	62.1	7.527
Japan	0.120	0.028	1.10	24.0	7.486
United Kingdom	0.201	0.240	1.41	119.0	7.117
Italy	0.191	0.039	0.46	20.7	6.492
Spain	0.082	0.011	0.20	13.2	5.329

Source: Ministry of Industry, Madrid.

Summarising, the Japanese model, used by some to justify the situation in Spain, is fundamentally different. Those who accuse Spain of *pereza empresarial* (entrepreneurial laziness) would appear closer to the truth, at least in certain sectors.

This situation has not escaped those responsible for innovation policy in Spain, who are trying to move from a defensive position to dynamic action. This policy consists in the first place of supporting the innovation process, wherever it can arise and develop. The different components of this policy appear in all the remaining chapters of this document. The accent here will be on measures to limit Spain's technological dependence.

The first requirement is to have reliable information about the *demand for foreign technology* in order to establish whether this is entirely justified – which it often is – or whether it stems from a certain "laziness" in the system. The *Registro de Contratos de Transparencia de Tecnologia* (register of technology transfer contracts) should be used as a basis for drawing up a policy. This implies that this register should be compiled on the basis of questionnaires simpler and richer in content than the existing ones, qualified as "prolix and inefficient". It also implies intercommunication through a joint computerised data base between all those involved in the process of authorising licences and contracts, in particular the General Directorate for Industrial Innovation and Technology and the General Directorate for Foreign Transactions.

It is wisely suggested in the Memorandum already cited that the *Registro de Exportacion de Tecnologia* (register of technology exports) and the *Registro de Adquisicion de Tecnologia* (register of technology acquisition) should be treated in the same fashion and come under the same authority. It is also suggested that links should be strengthened with the *Registro de la Propriedad Industrial* (register of industrial property rights) and with research centres.

The aim of obtaining this information should not be a purely negative action aimed at discouraging those applying for licences. On the contrary, it should make it possible to accelerate authorisation, bringing the waiting time from over five months down to one month in cases where the technology transfer is in fact justifiable. It should also make it possible to avoid buying abroad what is already available in Spain or what could be available within a reasonable period, even at the price of a considerable effort.

This implies that those responsible must have a perfect knowledge of the stock of results available and of the research possibilities.

It is in fact best not to wait for demand to appear but to try to anticipate it and prepare appropriate strategies. The Memorandum outlines a typical possible action concerning the suppliers of big foreign subsidiaries (e.g. in the automobile industry) which are characterised by the high cost of their foreign contracts. The idea of helping them, in particular by the automation and robotisation of their plant, should certainly be adopted.

The policy therefore has to deal with many individual cases, which implies considerable decentralisation. There is a programme for the introduction of new technologies in enterprises, which through contracts concluded between the Ministry for Industry and various bodies resulted in the creation of three centres (in Navarra, Barcelona and Madrid).

VI. INNOVATION SUPPORT SERVICES

A great number of activities often considered as subsidiary play an important role in development of innovation. These activities are very varied, hence the heterogeneity of this Chapter. By bringing them together, the Secretariat wishes to stress the fact that the innovation process does not require research and financing alone, but also a favourable general environment without which it has difficulty in developing.

These activities concern:

- Scientific, technical, economic and administrative information and documentation;
- The development of human resources in enterprises;
- Legal assistance and the protection of innovation;
- Tests, controls and standards.

Services to help the development of markets will be discussed below (Chapter VIII).

Working on the basis of the knowledge already acquired by man in the use of technologies – mainly the role of the engineer – or making it advance – the role of the researcher – it is essential that access to this knowledge should be easy.

The information conveying this knowledge must be available through a system that is comprehensive, selective, reliable and rapid.

There are a considerable number of statistical and bibliographical data bases in the world, over 1 500 of which are likely to interest researchers and innovators. Spain has an organisation, FUINCA (Computerised Scientific Information Network Foundation) which plays an important role in the diffusion of techniques, training of people and installation of terminals. At the end of 1983 there were 69 terminals in Spain.

As the situation is evolving rapidly, it is difficult to obtain an overview. To design an efficient policy in this area the replies to the following questions are required:

Is there in Spain a comprehensive policy for linking up with data banks throughout the world? Who is responsible for this policy?

How are the existing terminals distributed among universities, research centres, enterprises, organisations, intermediary bodies?

Such services are expensive. Who finances or subsidises their use?

The ideal would obviously be for each user to be able to work directly through a terminal connected to the major data banks. This implies time and training, hence the idea of intermediary bodies that can be attached to existing libraries or documentation centres or established on an *ad hoc* basis. Thus, in 1983 Navarra set up a technological information service open equally to individuals, public and private bodies and enterprises. This service is headed by a specialised analyst with a terminal connected to DIALOG and ESA, giving access to 350 data bases and 50 millions bibliographical references. There is also a microfilm and microfiche reader/copier.

41

The researcher and innovator work in a limited field, so that the data base they need is a very small subset of the enormous mass of data accessible throughout the world. The creation and updating of these subsets is essential to facilitate their work. In many countries, technological centres or trade associations perform this role of initial selection, building up a relevant and complete base meeting the needs of a given category of users, who generally access the secondary base directly in conversational mode. We have very little information about the existence of such data bases in Spain.

It is such data bases that can include information not considered worthy of incorporation in the big international data bases, but nevertheless essential because it reflects the local environment. Who is working on what in Spain, or in Navarra? What are the local markets? What is the legal and administrative framework?

Conversely, such scientific and technical information centres can inject data generated in Spain into the international network, which is important from the standpoint of the countries prestige and proof of its position as a fully-fledged partner. This linking of the local, regional, national and international levels of information merits in depth analysis.

The direct consultation of primary sources is not always essential, a selective synthesis of knowledge often being sufficient, at least in the early stages. There are many bodies publishing such syntheses.

Thus, the CDTI issues numerous publications in three series:

- AZUL series dealing with general problems in science and technology;
- AMARILLA series devoted to specific technological topics such as robotics;
- VERDE series devoted to specific industries.

The IMPI (Instituto de la Mediana y Pequena Empresa Industrial – Institute of Small and Medium Industrial Enterprises), which plays a role in the financing of enterprises, also publishes a monthly journal giving useful economic, financial, fiscal, legal, etc., information.

It seems that the publications of these two bodies (CDTI and IMPI) complement one another usefully. In addition, IMPI has branches in each Autonomous Community.

On the other hand, the universities and various research centres do not generally seem to give adequate reports of their activities.

Information of all kinds does not only circulate in printed or computerised form – seminars and symposiums play a very important role, sometimes associated with exhibitions. Though there is a lack of statistics on this type of meeting in Spain, it would appear that there are not enough of them. It is the role of learned societies, big research centres, research associations, etc., to organise them, not only at the national but also at regional level. It should also be noted that a possible means of stimulating these activities in the framework of higher education institutions consists in making available "mission-documentation" funds. It seems though that such a mechanism is not generally available.

The development of human resources in enterprises is a powerful factor for innovation if it is oriented towards creativity and not just limited to improving management capability. The IMPI encourages and subsidises numerous courses and seminars organised by chambers of commerce, federations and associations of enterprises.

In addition, local and regional bodies support numerous activities of this type which have the advantage, among others, of promoting meetings and discussions, as does the system of study grants and travel grants to attend congresses abroad, etc., allocated by a number of national and regional bodies (see Chapter IX).

Despite all the efforts to ensure the diffusion of useful information, the single inventor or small firm is often at a loss when faced with the complex tasks involved in developing the innovation, in particular the problems concerned with taking out patents and finding finance. Assistance is necessary here and could be provided by commercial advisory services; however, such services could also be provided by non-profit making bodies. The IMPI seems well placed to fill this role, as do a number of regional organisations assisting industry. This is not a question of financial aid, but of intellectual, technical, legal and administrative assistance.

As for the final development stage of an innovation it is necessary to conduct tests leading to a definition of the process and/or the product. This is often the role of a pilot installation designed, built and operated by an enterprise, for whom this can cause financial problems (see Chapter VII). In some cases, however, it suffices to have a few accurate measurements made by specialised laboratories, often test laboratories also responsible for standardization procedures. The documents available do not allow any evaluation of the measurement, control and test facilities existing in Spain, which are probably dispersed and decentralised.

The Bill on standardization and certification (1984) is aimed at enhancing the quality of industrial products, improving protection and defending enterprises against unfair competition. Its provisions should cover:

- The body responsible for standardization;
- The network of national test and calibration laboratories;
- Bodies co-operating with the administration;
- The authorities drawing up regulations;
- The service issuing conformity certificates;
- The test and inspection service.

The fact is that the whole of innovation protection policy is involved here. The problem of taking out patents will not be discussed in this document since Spain's entry to the EEC will mean a complete change in this respect. It should be noted, however, that computerisation (already achieved) of the patent register will help integration into the European system.

VII. FINANCIAL RESOURCES

Nothing can be done without money and the financing of enterprises is a major factor in development policy. The role of the banks is very important, but is limited by their concern with minimising risks. The evaluation of risk is based on analysis of the enterprise operations, but unfortunately those set up to launch an innovation are not in a position to reassure the banks and some other solution has to be found.

As regards existing enterprises wanting to develop an innovation, the problems vary considerably with size. Big firms often have a cash flow that allows them to launch new activities, and in any event they can always resort to the financial market, to obtain bank loans or to increase capital, or to issue bonds. However, it should be noted that these procedures are not applicable to *nationalised undertakings*, and INI and INH account for 10 per cent of Spain's industrial GDP. Many of the branches of the INI group are in serious financial difficulty, in particular through their lack of own funds which causes high financial charges. For these undertakings, the development of innovation requires – or is concomitant with – financial restructuring. It seems that a real strategy of financial reorganisation is being developed. This would need to take account of the innovation possibilities in the different industrial sectors.

Financing innovation in *small and medium enterprises* (SMEs) is more difficult because of their difficulty of access to the financial market, which has in any case had to meet constantly growing demands from the nationalised sector (which already took over 15 per cent in 1978). It is therefore necessary to develop secondary regional financial markets. This aspect does not seem to receive all the necessary attention.

This does not mean however, that SMEs should not try to provide guarantees to give lenders confidence in them. Spain has some interesting and novel mechanisms here.

The first is constituted by the *Mutual Guarantee Societies* (SGR) inspired by the French Sociétés de Crédit Mutuel. Their legal framework was fixed in July 1978. They are commercial undertakings of a mutualist nature, providing guarantees by endorsement (or any other legal form), any other type of intervention being excluded. The capital – which varies since the SGRs are open-ended – is provided by members and does not take the form of shares but of "quotas", the participation of members not being proportional to their contribution. (Each member has at least one vote and cannot hold more than 5 per cent of the votes.)

Members are of two types:

- "Protectors", who cannot ask for the SGR guarantee – these are generally public or private institutional bodies;
- "Participants", i.e. enterprises who can have recourse to the guarantee.

The SGRs build up a "guarantee fund", financed by members' contributions and the interest earned on them. The investment of these funds is subject to a number of rules (e.g. at least 20 per cent in public loans). The total of the debts guaranteed cannot exceed 25 times the capital fund plus earnings and the duration of guaranteed operations cannot exceed 12 years.

44

Obtaining the guarantee is not free – the different costs (investigation of the project, administrative costs, etc.) can amount to as much as 3 per cent of the guaranteed sum per year, which may appear high. At present total SGR capital must be in the region of Ptas 5 000 million.

If a member goes bankrupt, his debts are repaid first by the totality of his contribution, then the balance is taken from the contributions of other members according to a proportionality rule.

An additional mechanism necessary to the development of the SGRs is provided by a second guarantee (guarantee of a debt already guaranteed) given by the Mixed Second Guarantee Society where the State intervenes by defining in the budget law the total sum that can be guaranteed (Ptas 8 000 million in 1980). The system is complex, costly, limited in the amount that can be guaranteed and probably cumbersome in operation, but the idea is good.

There certainly remain difficulties to be resolved and one of the paths explored is the setting up of refinancing companies, such as the SOGASA founded in 1980. This interesting system appears to be rapidly evolving.

The SGRs are grouped in a Spanish confederation of SGRs, CESGAR. This might possibly be called upon to play the role of a second degree guarantee corporation.

Summarising, Spain has an interesting system for helping SMEs and its evolution is worth following closely.

The interest of the venture capital system has not escaped those responsible for economic development through innovation, who have closely studied the American model and its European derivatives, encouraged in this by a historic Spanish precedent – the financing of the expeditions of Christopher Columbus by Queen Isabel the Catholic.

The aim is the same as that expressed in 1946 by Senator R. Flanders, then head of the Federal Reserve Bank of Boston: to syphon off the inactive capital of insurance companies or any funds available for investment in favour of small and medium enterprises or new enterprises to enable them to exploit their ideas or research findings. The success of George Doriot's American Research and Development Corporation has certainly stimulated the thinking of Spanish Authorities.

What is required is an institutionalised financial activity aimed at providing permanent capital, but on a temporary and minority basis, generally accepting the risk of failure, to enterprises who want to develop thanks to innovations. A legal framework is obviously required, this being provided in the United States by the Small Business Investment Act of 1958 which gave rise to the Small Business Investment Companies, about half of whose activity consists of supplying venture capital. There are also numerous other companies supplying venture capital, bank subsidiaries, holdings, financial groups, etc.

This type of activity has developed more recently in Spain, with the creation of SEFINNOVA in 1976 by the Bank of Bilbao with the participation of other banks, savings banks, enterprises, and even the World Bank. Its registered capital was Ptas 465 million in 1983, and this was planned to be doubled.

Afterwards come the *Fomento de Inversiones Industriales*, whose activity seems to be limited, and the *Sociedad Bancaya de Promocion Empresarial*, which has not developed its venture capital activities very much.

In 1981, INI set up ENISA (Empresa Nacional de Innovacion) with a capital of Ptas one billion and a whole series of SODIS (Sociedades de Desarrollo Industrial) in connection with various financial and industrial groups for the different regions (SODIAN in Andalousia, SODICAN in the Canaries, etc.) It would be interesting to know how the regional development societies, set up as from 1970 to reduce inequalities between regions, have been involved in this process. More generally there is a need to update the somewhat obsolete data and determine trends. The most recent data are not always available in public documents.

The incentives for the creation of such companies are mainly tax incentives and operate at two levels:

- At the level of the venture capital companies themselves, who are encouraged to aim at capital appreciation;
- At the level of the companies assisted, whose investment should be encouraged.

Under the Decree Law of 27th December 1978, a very substantial share (up to 95 per cent) of the capital appreciation of venture capital company shares are not taxable, but it seems that there are restrictive conditions, in particular the fact that such companies should have the provision of venture capital as their only activity.

There are many ways in which venture capital companies operate, in particular:

a) Taking a shareholding through the creation and purchase of new shares. This is often accompanied by taking a post as administrator. Generally the "exit procedure" is provided for, i.e. the way in which the shares will be resold;
b) Subscribing for debentures. This system gives less guarantee for the supplier of the capital and no chance of substantial capital gain;
c) A mixed system with the debentures convertible into shares according to pre-arranged conditions;
d) There are also other possibilities, for example the rate of interest on debentures may be linked with the development of the enterprise. Spain has undoubtedly considered the solutions adopted in other countries and has probably developed some of its own, but the process of providing venture capital is still in its infancy and there are no statistics available.

It would be advisable in particular to identify which specific methods venture capital companies prefer.

Any venture capital financing mechanism implies an evaluation of the risk, or rather the chances of success and its possible extent. This evaluation has to be reliable, but also very rapid, speed of implementation often being vital to success. Venture capital companies therefore need to have their own specialists or access to outside specialists and modern methods of evaluation backed-up by global analyses and forecasts of market trends and future needs.

In addition, venture capital companies should be able to obtain from public or private sources the general basic studies and in particular forecasts – technological and socio-economic – that they need. Does a sufficient number of well documented studies exist?

It is obvious that if venture capital companies are to develop in Spain, this will result in a change in the structure of enterprises, obliged to be more transparent and to provide development plans and the role of certain minority shareholders will become more important. By and large, the level of reflection should be raised. The role of trade associations will probably become more important.

Venture capital companies are not the only answer to the problem of developing innovation in enterprises. The role of the CDTI, for example, has already been mentioned, but many other solutions are possible. Thus, one proposal has been that the government should oblige credit institutions to devote a (small) share of their loans to high-risk innovation operations.

The possible development of the bank's role in financing innovation requires to be studied further. The fact is that the question is really more general – it is a matter of deciding how to develop the spirit of enterprise among both potential entrepreneurs and among those who could participate in financing innovation. Since this question underlies all the problems studied in this document, it will not be formulated in general terms here. On the other hand, it is useful to raise a precise and specific problem, that of secondary stockmarkets:

Does the stockmarket in Spain meet modern requirements? Is there a need to develop secondary markets – regional markets, unlisted securities markets, etc.? By what methods?

The IMPI (Industrial SMEs Institute), set up in 1976, is an autonomous department of the Ministry for Industry and Energy which commenced its activities in 1978 when its aims and methods of intervention had been defined. It is in fact the arm of government that supports the action of developing SMEs.

Its first method of action is to promote the Mutual Guarantee Societies (SGR), in which it can participate as a "protector" member. As at the end of 1983, IMPI participated in about 30 SGRs and in SOGASA (the SGR Refinancing Society) and the Mixed Second Guarantee Society. The SGR system thus appears horrendously complicated. Certain financiers have – partly in jest – asked whether it is a matter of reducing the risk or multiplying the numbers taking a profit.

The IMPI also supports the "collective actions" of groups of small enterprises who join together for a technical, commercial or other project (joint services such as a computer centre, procurement centre, etc.). The IMPI can finance up to 45 per cent of the company created.

At the end of 1982, IMPI was participating in about 50 collective action companies grouping over 1 200 enterprises. IMPI can also pay part of the interest paid by an enterprise to a lending body. This is a flexible mechanism for providing soft loans.

Lastly, the role of IMPI as an aid to management, training, etc., was discussed in the previous Chapter. Thus IMPI has very diversified possibilities for action, but in fields where there are also many other actors.

How does IMPI react to the possible competition from other public or private bodies? Does its belonging to the Ministry for Energy and Industry give it the role of arbitrator?

Well designed *taxation* systems can play a significant incentive role for the development of innovation. As seen above (Chapter VII), tax advantages are offered to venture capital companies. What is the position for an enterprise carrying out research and wanting to innovate? The tax incentive here seems very modest and it is doubtful whether enterprises consider it adequate.

This tax incentive takes two forms:

– Possibility of reducing the company's taxable profits by 15 per cent of the intangible investment cost and 30 per cent of investment in fixed assets (*activos fijos*) used for research and innovation;
– Possibility of accelerated amortization for R & D investment, i.e. five years for capital equipment and intangibles and seven years for buildings.

VIII. THE DEVELOPMENT OF MARKETS

The market economy has laws of its own and it often turns out that government action has the opposite effect to that desired. Measures therefore need to be flexibly and cautiously applied. This seems to be Spain's approach with the role of State purchases, which are to be stepped up and better oriented, and with the different types of export aid. The problem of customs tariffs will not be discussed here because Spain's entry to the EEC will completely change the situation.

Government markets in the defence field could play an important locomotive role. This is not yet the case, but close co-operation is planned between three Ministries – Defence, Education and Science, Industry and Energy – which should result in specific R&D programmes. Although important this is not enough in itself.

There are in fact many cases where well-placed defence orders can create a market for high value added products which subsequently spill over into the civil sector. This was the case in the United States for vitroceramics, many silicones and certain elastomers capable of withstanding harsh conditions. This is tantamount to including criteria concerning the possible civil spin-off in the criteria determining the choices for military expenditure. It is to be hoped that such expenditure fits at least partly into a national development plan, despite the legitimate concern with secrecy. The need for secrecy should not be exaggerated and should certainly not be used, as the humorist put it, to hide the fact ... that there is nothing to hide.

There are many other government markets which can play a locomotive role, however, in particular those concerning transport, various infrastructures and even education. The regulations concerning government markets were introduced 35 years ago and are obsolete.

There is no overall planning of government purchases and Spanish industrial firms often find themselves confronted with calls for tenders with short delivery times that they cannot meet, while certain foreign firms are equipped for such cases.

There is no centralisation, or at least co-ordination of purchases, which results in fragmentation of markets so that they rarely reach the critical mass necessary to have a locomotive effect. If care is not taken, the present process of regionalisation can only aggravate this fragmentation.

There is no mechanism to allow the purchase of prototypes. Choice of the contractor is often made according to catalogue, which obviously favours foreign firms.

In certain government markets the concept of "national producer" should be replaced by that of "national industrial effort".

The above, very general, remarks are taken from the Plan for Electronics and Informatics. Its authors are quite rightly concerned with this problem, particularly acute in the case of new technologies which lack the guarantees offered by standardization, certification, etc.

The opinions of the Plan for Electronics and Informatics on this subject should be taken into account not only in the framework of the plan itself but more generally as regards the overall role of government markets and the mechanisms by which contracts are awarded.

The Spanish State is also an industrialist via the INI. These nationalised industries invest. Their choice of capital equipment is governed by considerations of profitability and it is difficult to make them play a locomotive role in an innovation promotion policy. Nevertheless, the structure of the INI should permit:

- Collaboration between the different sectors of the nationalised enterprises to define common needs and the performance standards for equipment in general use (e.g. pumps) or specialised equipment;
- The establishment of incentive systems for suppliers;
- Promotion and financial support of research on materials and equipment.

All this is not so much a matter of legislation as of a way of looking at things that is not widespread enough at present.

It is not enough, however, to create and/or develop a national innovation market. It is also necessary to make Spanish innovations known, and to develop foreign markets for them. The cost of developing a market may be too great for small and medium firms, but there are a number of possible solutions existing in Spain:

- Support for groups of firms;
- Contribution to the cost of market research;
- Partial or total subsidisation of the cost of exhibiting in specialised foreign fairs.

Concerning this last type of intervention, it should be noted that there are mechanisms at both national and regional level (Navarra in particular) for the establishment of group stands, the effectiveness of which has been demonstrated. Spain is still poorly represented in international fairs, however, with the possible exception of those held in Spanish-speaking countries.

In the various documents available to the Secretariat, there is no mention of the possible role of embassy services (in particular the scientific and commercial services). Embassies are well placed for defining the sectors that could be occupied, and hence the innovations to be promoted, and the procedures to be adopted. It is necessary to "mobilise" embassies in this direction.

IX. THE IMPACT OF REGIONALISATION

In the industrialised countries, a scientific and technical policy oriented towards innovation is generally characterised by two very different aspects, one organised, with its own logic and fitting into a neat organisation chart, the other confused, made up of a multitude of mechanisms complementing one another and adjusting to one another. Numerous links are established between the two structures either through systems of collaboration or through financing procedures.

The process of decentralisation, long solidly installed in Germany, and developing in France and Spain, tends to multiply the problems of relations between decision-making systems at different levels and with different objectives.

The risk of duplication of effort is increased. Admittedly, this has its advantages from the creativity standpoint, since it gives rise to a certain emulation but financial resources are limited and their use needs to be optimised.

Decentralisation brings research closer to the user and hence favours the innovation process. Conversely, it aggravates competition in new fields, increasing the risk for the firms involved.

Among the documents available the Secretariat has not found any description of the principles on which tasks are allocated between the national, regional and local levels, and certainly no map of the geographical organisation of research and development efforts. This lack of a plan may turn out to be costly. Obviously, care has to be taken not to freeze structures and create rigid frameworks, but the general principles ought to be identified and formulated.

The example of Catalonia

Catalonia has an interdepartmental research and technological innovation commission (CIRIT) whose role is to encourage, promote and develop all research and innovation initiatives of interest to the region. This commission is at the highest regional government level (i.e. *la Generalitat*) where all interested departments are represented – education, energy policy, rural environment, promotion and development, the electricity undertaking (ENHER), various Catalan firms, etc.

The Commission's activities include:

- Training, through the awarding of grants, possibly for courses abroad or for preparing a thesis;
- Scientific infrastructures, by subsidising equipment and libraries;
- Research itself through subsidising projects;
- Stimulating the spirit of research and innovation by organising courses and conferences, supporting journals, young people's associations, etc.

The Commission has a scientific and technological Council (CCT) whose policy gives preference to three lines of research:

- Genetic engineering and biotechnologies;
- Micro-electronics;
- Global studies of ecosystems.

While this last poses no problems of co-ordination – the work on the ecosystems of the Ebro delta is remarkable and, of course, specific to Catalonia – the two others are also dealt with at national level. However one may wonder whether there are adequate institutional or informal links between the CCT and the bodies responsible for national scientific and technological policy, and, connected with this whether any cases of joint financing of projects by national bodies and the CCT have been identified.

The example of Catalonia is representative of a regional effort directed at:

- Improving the local physical and human potential;
- Carrying out complementary research to meet local needs;
- Carrying out research of national interest requiring co-ordination at the level of national research and innovation policy.

General problems

The *Navarra Official Bulletin* of July 1982 published some "Standards" for short-term industrial policy measures and measures to support investment and employment, approved by the Plenum of the Local Parliament. One section is entirely devoted to research and technological development. It suffices to follow the plan of this section to discover the seven general problems that warrant examination.

a) Information

Access to information will be facilitated for researchers and enterprises through:

- The installation of terminals connected to information networks;
- Publication of works on technological research topics in order to facilitate the spread of research findings and the opening of new paths.

The first point fits in with the logic of Chapter VI, but the second could lead to a waste of effort through duplication. As it happens the risk is not great – many publications need to be adapted to local needs and real duplication is less frequent than might be thought.

These services will be charged for, but may be more or less subsidised and in any case the charge would never be higher than the actual cost. This financial aspect of regional action is certainly a regulating instrument.

b) Training researchers

The regional authority can, in a regulatory framework yet to be defined:

- Award applied research grants to people resident for at least two years;
- Subsidise stays (of less than three months) in other research centres;
- Encourage active participation in congresses through subsidies;
- Help research-workers to follow advanced training courses;
- Organise or finance courses, seminars, etc.

There are obvious advantages in regionalising such activities, but by definition the research population is, or should be, mobile. The criteria for belonging to the region should not be too rigid. It is also necessary to avoid certain types of competition between the different systems of grants.

c) Assistance with the establishment of infrastructures

It seems that the regional authority's activity here is limited to interest-free loans covering up to 70 per cent of the equipment and apparatus necessary to the *private sector* for certain projects and complementary subsidies for centres installed on its territory. The risk of duplication of effort is therefore reduced. However, it is by no means certain that this approach optimises the utilisation of national and regional public funds in the absence of any co-ordination mechanisms.

d) Studies, research projects, pilot plants

Total or partial subsidies, interest-free loans, loans repayable if the project is sucessful (according to conditions laid down in advance), etc. – all these possibilities were provided for in the Navarra Standards mentioned above, so here we find a typical case where the central government and regional authority are trying to do the same thing. It seems that no principles have been laid down to try to better define the respective roles of the different authorities.

e) Product standardization and certification

If this is a means of providing local enterprises with the means of carrying out tests and enabling them to benefit from controls and advice, the measures envisaged by Navarra will be useful. If, as there is reason to fear, a local standardization process should arise, no overall policy would be possible in a field of particular importance for the protection and promotion of innovation.

f) Aid with selling technology abroad

Navarra wants to help enterprises exhibit at foreign fairs (see Chapter VIII) thanks to group stands, as well as to help with obtaining approval certification and foreign patents. On this last point, where very specialised competence is required, it is doubtful that regional mechanisms can be effective. It would be better to have powerful national mechanisms, public or private, regional aid being limited to a financial contribution and/or the creation of intermediary regional bureaux.

g) Formation of innovation societies and promotion of joint action

This covers the methods of financing studied in Chapter VII. The diversity of mechanisms is desirable, but excessive tax disparities between regions is to be avoided.

Thus, the text of the Navarra Standards brings out clearly the advantages of regional dynamism but also suggests that certain types of action need to be co-ordinated at national level, which will in any case be required by Spain's entry to the EEC. One can but ask a general question:

In the field of Spanish innovation policy, is there any project for a charter of relations between regional and central authorities or any equivalent document?

X. THE BIG SECTORAL PROGRAMMES

A scientific and technical policy cannot concentrate on all fields at once. Even if only for budgetary reasons such a policy is necessarily selective. This does not mean, however, that it should leave certain fields aside altogether. It has to endeavour to maintain everywhere, or almost everywhere, the necessary minimum level to assure the competence necessary for freedom of future choice. At very least it is a matter of keeping certain scientific and technological activities ticking over. No miracles are to be expected, but the importance of this must not be underestimated in the modern world.

In other fields, scientific and technological policy (STP) aims at maintaining a level of effort such that the chances of making discoveries are not too remote and that creativity can develop with reasonable hope of success.

In yet other fields, scientific and technological policy decides on a special effort, doing everything possible to achieve noteworthy results. These are the fields of *national interest* or *priority sectors*.

This is not the place to analyse the criteria for defining such sectors, which are in fact numerous, but one of them merits special mention in this document devoted to innovation policy – this is precisely the criterion of *probability of leading to an innovation*. Some of the programmes already mentioned, especially among the co-ordinated concerted projects, satisfy this criterion.

This brings us to the meeting point – the field of interaction – of science and technology policy and economic development policy, the two being distinct but more or less closely interconnected. Economic development policy like science and technology policy cannot make the same effort everywhere. It has to determine *priority sectoral action*, and here there may be more or less emphasis on the research and innovation effort. The fact is that experience shows that it is dangerous to let this drop below a certain level. A new industry can certainly be started using imported technologies, but in order to avoid total economic dependence it is necessary to be able to adapt and develop these technologies and at a later stage at least partly replace them by processes developed within the country.

The question therefore arises of whether the priority sectoral efforts in Spain take account of this necessary linkage with innovation policy. The Secretariat does not have complete data except on the National Plan for Electronics and Informatics. This plan is therefore taken as the main example, other areas being analysed more briefly afterwards.

The National Plan for Electronics and Informatics (PEIN) appears very satisfactory at first sight. It includes a medium term scenario (1987) which is really a short term horizon and scarcely more than an extrapolation of market trends, then a detailed programme broken down by branch with proposals for general measures concerned with financing, taxation, exports, etc.

The sectoral breakdown consists of plans for:

– Micro-electronics;
– Consumer electronics;

53

- Components;
- Telecommunications;
- Computers;
- Defence electronics;
- Industrial electronics;
- Electromedicine.

This breakdown will not be discussed here. The merit of the analysis is that it constitutes a generalised market study and fixes the roles of the different ministries in the development of the market. It is known, for example, that the Ministry of Education has a twofold role since it both trains people and buys equipment, so that it contributes in two ways to the extension of the market. However, the possible role of research is implied throughout this section.

Fortunately, however, a programme with a horizontal breakdown is also proposed, with plans for the diffusion of technology, factory siting, government purchases and, of particular interest for this report, a *research and development plan*, specifying the sums to be allocated to the different sectors for R&D in 1984, 1985 and 1986 *by the CAICYT* (a total of Ptas 3 800 million) and *the CDTI* (a total of Ptas 6 250 million), and announcing that the future Bill on research is to establish a co-ordination mechanism between science and technology policy and economic development policy.

The plan also provides for the creation of a micro-electronics R&D Centre based on existing resources in the CSIC and the private sector.

In this Chapter there is also a taxation measure – the right to deduct a certain percentage of R&D expenditure from taxable profits.

All this is no doubt useful, but the essentially quantitative and short-term nature of the Plan casts some doubt on its real effectiveness.

This is a rapidly evolving field that needs to be considered in the longer term, a dimension missing from the Plan. It is also necessary to have an inventory of Spanish R&D resources in this field, with an indication of strong and weak points and the chances of obtaining original results at least on certain specific problems.

The impression thus is that there has not been all the possible and desirable interaction between the policy for science and technology and the National Plan for Electronics and Informatics. This is regrettable, but can perhaps be explained by the backwardness of R&D in this sector.

There are certainly other sectoral plans in Spain, probably reflected in the programmes already mentioned such as aquaculture, agro-energy, biotechnology, etc., but it is a striking fact that some of these programmes – such as aquaculture – have been virtually unable to take off because of a lack of suitable infrastructures.

In fact few fields of economic development appear to have been studied in as much detail as that covered by the PEIN. The picture that emerges from the texts alone suggests that the science and technology policy and the economic development policy are not sufficiently mature for the necessary interactions to have developed.

XI. THE NEW LEGAL FRAMEWORK

At the beginning of this document, reference was made to the draft Memorandum for the Preparation of a Bill on the Development and Co-ordination of Scientific and Technological Research. This Memorandum, used extensively by the Secretariat in the preparation of this report, appeared in a considerably expanded version at the end of 1984.

Through this new version it is possible to get an idea of the probable new legal framework in which research and innovation will develop and to estimate the likely extent of progress. The present system, which developed spontaneously but which remains very inadequate as regards human and material resources, seems to lack the mechanisms required for proper co-ordination and rational decision-making. Some mechanisms do of course exist, perhaps too many even, but their role is not always clearly defined and a comprehensive reform is necessary.

The Memorandum seems to provide for three Acts and a number of *specific measures*. Considering these measures first, the most important are:

- The creation of an *ad hoc* Interministerial Commission, representing all the ministries concerned, its main role being to establish close and direct collaboration between the General Directorates for Scientific Policy on the one hand and Industrial Innovation and Technology on the other, thus providing a solution to a cause for concern mentioned several times in this report;
- Administrative reorganisation of the CAICYT and CDTI, to make them more effective and put them in closer touch with socio-economic reality.

For the CAICYT, the procedures mentioned above – "research projects", "concerted research plans", "R&D programmes", etc., – are defined, as is the launching of two centres, one for biotechnology, the other for micro-electronics.

The CSIC see its financial and human potential increased (200 more researchers) and the CDTI's budget increased by 71.3 per cent in 1984 over 1983.

- Agreements are to be concluded between the Ministry for Industry and Energy and the Industrial Councils of the Autonomous Communities;
- There is provision for the development of the "network of technological services" providing advice, training and even financing for enterprises.

The Act on University Reform improves the status and method of recruitment of university teachers (giving established status to 5 000 more people), fixes functioning by departments and makes research contracts concluded with outside bodies official.

The Act on Patents redefines the patentability criteria and solves the delicate problem of "proof" with regard to copying, fixes the conditions for admission to the body of patent agents, etc.

The most important is obviously the future *Act on the Development and Co-ordination of Scientific and Technological Research*, which in fact has two very different aspects that will be dealt with separately, one institutional and one scientific and technological, in effect the programme of work.

The intentions of the legislator regarding the institutional aspect are clear – to distinguish clearly the levels of research co-ordination, programming and execution, to correctly structure the bodies operating at each level and to define relations between the Central Government and the Autonomous Communities. The legislator also provides for the development of a single, homogeneous status for researchers.

In accordance with this logic there therefore appear:

- *A general Council for Science and Technology* – the body responsible for the dovetailing of national and regional policies;
- *An Interministerial Commission for Scientific Research and Technological Development* – the supreme body for programming, setting priorities and co-ordinating efforts; it has the financial power.

The CAICYT is to be integrated into the body preparing decisions (*La Unidad de Apoyo*) of the Commission.

The CSIC, The Nuclear Energy Commission, etc., see their status defined – these are the bodies actually executing the programmes.

This project (still somewhat imprecise) is rational, but cannot be judged until the details are known. As an example of the uncertainty remaining it is not clear whether, or how, those responsible for the executing bodies wil be associated in the programming decisions. For the moment, one can but note a serious omission, the *lack of an overall view of the system for carrying out technological research and planning its development*. This is the major weakness of the Memorandum and must be corrected.

It was logical that programming procedures should be included in the Bill – definitions of national and sectoral programmes (though the difference is sometimes arbitrary), frameworks for their design, etc. The dominant impression is that this is a flexible programming system allowing the government to intervene on a large scale where this is necessary, without blocking the initiatives of ministries or national research bodies when these are in line with the general interest. Used properly, this method can work very effectively.

Was it necessary to go into the details of these programmes in the Bill? The temptation is to answer in the negative because a programme is by definition evolutive and limited in time and thus should not be a matter for the law. The impression is that the authors of the project wanted to use the possible content of research activities as an argument in favour of the reform, making it credible by showing what it will make possible.

There are certainly other ways of proving that the reform is necessary and it is probably dangerous to combine it with a necessarily incomplete programme that is certainly open to criticism. The lack of such topics as water resource management, technologies of the habitat, urban problems, etc., will certainly provoke reaction. Similarly, putting the accent on aquaculture without situating it in the general context of the problems of food production may give rise to argument. In other words, the presentation of this section of the Bill will require some caution. But that is a question that has little to do with the problem of developing a spirit of innovation, which should appear everywhere, whether or not there is a programme.

CONCLUSIONS

While creativity develops mainly – but not exclusively – in the context of pure and applied research, innovation has to develop throughout the socio-economic fabric. However, the process of innovation, what stimulates it and what impedes it, is poorly understood. Thus, paradoxically, the big technical ministries (Industry, Agriculture, etc.) aiming at progress through innovation are those that ought to devote most attention to sociological phenomena. Spain, because of its entry to the EEC and the considerable effort it is making to modernise its research and production infrastructure is at present a melting pot for reflection on the sociological/technological/economic interfaces, making it a particularly interesting case for analysis.

In particular, it will be very instructive to see how the extremely apt and forcefully expressed idea of the Ministry for Industry and Energy's General Directorate for Industrial Innovation and Technology works out in practice: "We must opt for close co-ordination at the planning level (fixing objectives), less in the management phase (mobilising resources) and none in the execution stage (where the maximum of initiatives appear)." These words are those of Florencio Ornia (with those in brackets added by the Secretariat), Director General, who came down heavily in favour of the *co-ordinated-concerted system.*

It will also be interesting to see how innovation develops in agriculture where the ideas generally arise in a context – research – very far removed from that of the users – rural areas.

Lastly the Bill seems to give priority, which is normal, almost exclusively, which would be a mistake, to the role of two ministries – Education and Industry. The small space devoted in the Memorandum to the problems of innovation in agriculture, public works and transport is disturbing. It certainly reflects present differences in dynamism between sectors, but the Bill should take a broader and longer view.

57

Annex I

SOME BASIC STATISTICAL DATA FOR SPAIN

Area: 504 800 sq. km

Major cities   :

–	Madrid (capital)	3 000 000	
–	Barcelona	2 000 000	inhabitants
–	Valencia	800 000	approximately
–	Sevilla	700 000	

Currency   :   peseta; 1 $ = 132.40 pesetas at 31.12.86

Languages   :   national official: castillan
regional official: basque, catalan, galician

	Unit	1965	1975	1983
Demography[1]				
Population	million	32.1	35.6	38.1
Density	inhab./sq.km	64	71	75.5
Annual growth	%	1.0	1.1	0.7[a]
Infant mortality	0/00	37.3	18.9	9.6[a]
Life expectancy	years	69	73	74[b]
Urban population	%	61	71	75[b]
Culture				
Illiteracy	%	9.8	7.6	6.8[c]
Number of physicians	0/00 inhab.	1.3	1.8	2.6[b]
Schooling Second level[e]	%	38	73.0	88[b]
Third level	%	5.6	20.4	23[d]
TV sets (estimated)	0/00	55	187	254
Published books	titles	17 342	23 527	24 569[c]

1.   *a* = 1982; *b* = 1981; *c* = 1979; *d* = 1980; *e* = 11-17 years.
Source: «Statistics of OECD Member Countries», 1987 edition, *OECD Observer*, No. 145, April/May 1987; *L'Etat du Monde 1984*, éditions La Découverte, Paris, 1984.

Annex II

STATISTICAL DATA ON FOREIGN TRADE[1]

	Unit	1965	1975	1983
	% GDP	8.5	11.4	15.4
Total imports[a]	$ billion	3.0	16.2	29.2
Agricultural products	%	26.8	21.4	15.3[b]
Energy products	%	10.0	26.0	40.0[b]
Other mineral products	%	4.0	5.2	4.1[b]
Total exports[b]	$ billion	1.0	7.7	19.7
Agricultural products	%	51	23.6	32.2[b]
Mineral products[c]	%	2.0	1.3	2.0[b]
Industrial products	%	41.9	71.8	52.3[b]
Main suppliers	% imports			
EEC		37.4	34.7	32.4
Middle-East		5.8	18.3	16.1
United States		17.4	15.9	11.8
Main clients	% exports			
EEC		35.7	44.7	48.3
Africa		5.3	9.8	10.9
Latin america	11.0	9.9	6.1	

1. a = goods; b = 1982; c = not including petroleum products.
Source: L'Etat du Monde 1984, éditions La Découverte, Paris, 1984.

ECONOMIC STATISTICS[1]

	Unit	1965	1975	1983
GDP	$ billion	23.4	104.8	158.3
Annual growth	%	7.5[c]	3.8[b]	2.3
Per inhabitant	$	730	2 950	5 316[g]
Structure of GDP[e]				
Agriculture	%	16.3	9.9	6.1[e]
Industry	%	38.6	39.5	33.7[e]
Services	%	45.1	50.6	60.2[e]
Inflation rate	%	5.6[c]	18.3[d]	12.2
Active population	million	..	12.4	13.1[e]
Agriculture	%	33.6	21.3	16.0[e]
Industry	%	35.9	38.0	33.4[e]
Services	%	30.6	39.6	43.2[e]
Unemployment[a]	%	1.3	4.7	18.0
Public expenditure				
Education	% PIB	0.9	1.6	2.6[f]
Defence	% PIB	3.4	2.6	2.1[e]
Energy				
Production	million TEC	16.0	18.5	25.6[e]
Consumption	million TEC	32.7	76.5	86.8[e]

1. *a* = end of year; *b* = average 1971-80; *c* = average 1961-70; *d* = average 1974-78; *e* = 1982; *f* = 1979; *g* = in 1979-81 dollars and exchange rate for the same year; TEC = ton equivalent of coal.
Source: *L'Etat du Monde 1984*, éditions La Découverte, Paris, 1984.

NOTES AND REFERENCES

1. The recent Science and Technology Bill which is discussed in the Examiners' Report, provides for CAYCIT to be abolished and for its personnel and equipment to be transferred to the Permanent Commission created by the corresponding Act.

2. The figure of 24 000 includes all categories of professors as well as teaching assistants. Many of them hold precarious contracts. Ten years ago the corresponding number was of only 8 000.

3. The National Centre for Micro-electronics Research and Development and the National Centre for Biotechnology are both centres of the CSIC in which various universities participate.

Part II

EXAMINERS' REPORT

Mr. Pierre Piganiol,
Rapporteur,
Former Délégué à la Recherche,
France

Mr. Konrad Ratz,
Director,
Fund for Research Promotion
Vienna, Austria

Mr. Benjamin Huberman,
Former Deputy Director of the Office
for Scientific and Technological Policy
at the White House, Washington DC,
United States

I. INTRODUCTION

Spain's forthcoming entry into the Common Market has engendered a strong political will to intensify the country's research effort and to support innovation. This has been reflected in wide-ranging analysis of the present situation and in the development of a whole set of decisions, most of which have been embodied in a Bill.

The Evaluation Group has not been able to consider results of a policy which was formulated only recently, and has not yet been put into application. Instead the Group has:

- Assessed the qualities and shortcomings of the present situation;
- Considered the appropriateness of the measures proposed to improve it;
- Identified certain additional measures as being necessary.

The Evaluation Group began by noting a number of facts which are definite advantages for Spain and which warrant reasonable optimism as to the outcome of the government's efforts.

These include, above all, a manifest awareness in the highest government circles, in the universities and in industry, of the vital role of research and innovation and of their essential contribution to the future.

The fact that a Bill has been drafted, together with Spain's request for an OECD review of the policy she is contemplating, demonstrates that she has well understood the problems before her, and that she intends to solve them.

Beyond this, Spain possesses an outward-looking university and industrial base which constitutes a firm point of departure, while her liberal attitude towards foreign investment facilitates technology transfers.

Another asset is her natural propensity – a cultural phenomenon – to respond to incentives from the hierarchical top. This means that policies formulated by the government will be pursued and will bear fruit: all that is required is to be more vigorous and judicious than in the past.

Lastly, regionalisation in Spain, although fraught with certain dangers as discussed below, should enable general policy decisions to be realistically tailored to local conditions.

Nevertheless, Spain does have certain handicaps which the new policy should help to overcome. These are analysed in detail below. In fact, three major shortcomings arise in various forms:

- Qualitative and quantitative shortcomings in the scientific and technological infrastructure and in the financial resources for running it;
- The lack of a well co-ordinated network of decision centres with well defined remits;
- A general climate that is inadequately favourable to innovation.

This report has been constructed to reflect the differing agents involved rather than the kinds of problem to be tackled. This does make for some repetition, but has the advantage of grounding the report in Spain's scientific and technological framework as it really is today, so that all those with a part to play in implementing the new policy will easily find the review and recommendations which concern them.

The recommendations are set out in the course of each chapter according to the problems at issue, and are displayed within insets to distinguish them from the general text of the report.

II. THE ROLE OF THE UNIVERSITIES

A university can intervene in the innovation process in several ways:
- By training future innovators;
- By providing the country with the basic scientific and technological knowledge it requires;
- By providing a centre of skill and competence widely available to all who may have need of it;
- By making discoveries and inventions, thus providing points of departure for the development of innovations.

Training designed to develop the capacity to innovate cannot be confined to theory and to the lecture hall. It must be supported by a substantial amount of practical activity and extended by research involvement, i.e. training via research.

For lack of statistics it is hard to assess the amount of funding earmarked for practical exercises. But several informants suggest that it is not enough, and that shortages of equipment are impairing quality in education.

Recommendation No. 1 *A substantial increase should be provided in funding of practical work in higher education. This recommendation also applies to secondary education (first and second cycles).*

The first goal of university research is to ensure the quality of professional teaching, derived from direct contact with the science being taught. Every professor should be able to carry out the kind of research he himself needs for a better understanding of his subject.

This research can be most conveniently carried out in a laboratory associated with university chair. Other arrangements are possible though, and what matters is that every teacher should be in a position freely to engage in his or her preferred research.

Recommendation No. 2 *Adequate research funds should be made available to each teacher, whether he has a laboratory of his own or is accommodated in an outside laboratory.*

Where a laboratory is associated with a chair, its profitability should be maximised. The laboratory should therefore be in a position to work:
- For a national programme of systematic basic research;
- For industrial requirements under contract.

The first point will be examined later; the second is covered in the Bill, which is designed to ensure a happy integration of all university laboratories within the overall national research framework.

III. THE ROLE OF THE HIGHER COUNCIL
FOR SCIENTIFIC RESEARCH (CSIC)

The CSIC is a most important body comprising a complex of very different kinds of laboratories and institutes, which cannot therefore be easily assigned any single well-defined mission. It is concerned with both basic and applied research, though in the latter field it is probably too remote from market reactions and requirements whether in agriculture or in industry.

Logically, the CSIC should become the essential tool for systematic basic research, fundamental in character and "upstream" of applied research activities in the public sector.

These latter should be consolidated into coherent groups, each group related to a well-defined field. This is a necessary condition if the sectors to be served – each comprising essentially a collection of small enterprises (in farming, building, etc.) – are to have adequate laboratory resources.

The CSIC, as part of its mission in support of systematic basic research, should maintain close contacts with the university world – so as to identify and select the most promising research fields – and with industry leaders so as to determine in which fields the development of basic understanding is most needed for the progress of applications, and hence of innovation.

The CSIC should also place contracts with university laboratories, in order to derive maximum benefit from them by putting them to work on the whole range of programmed basic research in addition to their own discretionary research.

Lastly, the CSIC should be able to accommodate independent research by teachers without their own laboratories, and to provide facilities (under contract with industry), for the basic research necessary for the development of specific projects.

Recommendation No. 3   *The role of the CSIC should be strengthened by mandating it to cover the whole range of basic research that the country needs, whether in universities, agriculture or industry. It would be desirable to integrate the applied research centres of the CSIC with associated research units of specific ministries.*

University research and CSIC research thus combined would constitute a remarkable potential and would provide Spain with an infrastructure for high-level basic research and for training larger numbers of high-grade scientists and technologists.

As for the transfer of applied research activities this would obviously include the transfer of associated resources as well as research staff. Clearly the latter may create difficulties which will require appropriate incentives to overcome. Once the transfers have been made it will be necessary to assure effective co-ordination between fundamental and applied research.

IV.   SCIENCE POLICY WITHIN
THE MINISTRY OF EDUCATION AND SCIENCE (MEC)

This Ministry formerly had its own unit, the Advisory Commission for Scientific and Technological Research (CAICYT), which the new Bill does not mention[1]. Yet the Ministry does need such a unit if it is to accomplish the following tasks as laid down *within the framework set by the Interministerial Commission*:

- Development of independent research in universities;
- Regular listing and publication of project details and results;
- Formulation of policy for systematic basic research;
- Arranging for this to be performed by the CSIC, where necessary in co-operation with other agencies outside the Ministry;
- Accepting public and private research contracts insofar as they do not risk jeopardising the specific functions of the universities and the CSIC;
- Approving and co-ordinating international co-operative agreements for basic research.

All these activities should of course be submitted for examination, modification and approval by the Interministerial Commission. But that Commission clearly could not carry out all the necessary preliminary work by itself.

Two solutions are possible:

- Maintaining the CAICYT alongside the CSIC;
- Merging the two.

The first would have the advantage of following on from the present situation. But it would be cumbersome: furthermore the CSIC, as a major research establishment, would have a budget of its own which it ought then to be able to control. The merger approach would have the effect of providing the CSIC with a powerful and efficient governing body.

Recommendation No. 4   *An agency with the function of formulating an overall plan for the development of basic research, for submission to the Interministerial Commission, should be provided for and, if possible, included in the text of the Bill.*

Such a body should of course receive input both from the country's best scientists and from those directly aware of the basic research requirements in their own lines of research. The body should therefore include representatives from the applied research laboratories of other ministries, even from certain industrial laboratories.

V. THE ROLE OF THE MINISTRY FOR INDUSTRY AND ENERGY (MINER)

What has been described above would be intended to provide the country with the overall range of basic knowledge required. This is essential, but must inevitably be situated "upstream" of the innovation process (which is not of course to rule out the emergence of innovations from MEC research, though it would not be MEC that would develop them).

Major responsibility for the development of innovation in industry falls on the MINER. It should be remarked that senior MINER officials who met the Evaluation Group were fully aware of this problem and determined to solve it. Their assessment is excellent: they recognise the twofold need to establish a solid infrastructure and to stimulate positive attitudes towards innovation. The OECD must warmly endorse that approach.

By *infrastructure* is meant sufficient human and material research resources devoted to industrial innovation. The resources need to be linked with industries, most of which are not doing enough research of their own. Furthermore, the practice in United States industry of appointing a Vice-President specifically responsible for research is virtually unknown in Spain.

The industrial fabric in Spain is complex; its many strands include:

– The large nationalised industries grouped together in the INI;
– Large private industries, many of them subsidiaries of multinationals;
– Small and medium-sized firms (SMEs);
– An efficient individual craftsman sector, though much of this, especially in the building trades, would benefit from integration into more conventional enterprises.

Desirable new measures differ in each of the above cases.

Public sector industries are experiencing considerable (short-term and structural) difficulties. Restructuring them will be expensive and there is some risk that the essential financial commitment will crowd out, or at least delay, what is also needed for the private sector, especially SMEs.

Recommendation No. 5   *It will not be enough to put public sector industries on a sounder financial footing. Their laboratories should be developed and supported only insofar as genuinely innovative programmes are proposed. The Centre for Industrial Technological Development (CDTI) (see below) will have an important role to play here.*

Recommendation No. 6   *Efforts and commitments towards public sector industries (which are indispensable) should be accompanied by equal efforts and commitments to the private industrial sector.*

Private sector industries, especially SMEs, should develop their experimental and research resources. This presupposes their own adequate capitalisation (relying on private savings which must be stimulated and mobilised) and suitable cash flows (by means of appropriate fiscal policies). There should also be special incentives to support their own research efforts.

Recommendation No. 7   *Fiscal incentives should be developed in conjunction with increased availability of venture capital to encourage firms to invest in research.*

Recommendation No. 8   *It is desirable to increase the proportion of government-funded research carried out by firms under contract. Each contract should provide for an additional amount of about 10 per cent to strengthen the general resources of the industrial laboratory.*

In every enterprise of sufficient size, the "research and development" function should be clearly identified, and in the hands of highly qualified personnel whose leaders hold very high positions in the firm's hierarchy (the American "Vice-President in charge of Research" formula). Such structures are rare in Spain: however good examples do exist in several industries with high scientific content (e.g. pharmacy) and the successes to be derived from such a system – notably in export performance – should encourage many more firms to follow the same line.

Lastly, MINER should assist innovation projects in firms via the CDTI, whose role seems so important that it will be treated in a separate section (see Chapter VI).

Not all firms are large enough for their research effort to reach the critical size for prospects of success.

Recommendation No. 9   *It is essential that every firm, however small, should have access to the research resources necessary for its future success.*

The CDTI offers part of the solution to this problem (see below) but will have difficulty in completing its mission if the technological research infrastructure remains in its present condition. It will be useful here to draw attention to the approaches of other industrialised countries, and to set out their advantages and shortcomings. It is for the various individuals responsible for technological development in Spain to choose the most suitable solution in each case:

a)   All the members of a particular industry contribute to the establishment and operation of a joint laboratory, where problems of interest to the industry generally are resolved, and also where work is done under contract on problems of individual members. This solution is difficult to implement, because it requires the agreement of a great many firms about the kind of investment to be made and the programmes to be pursued. There are nevertheless good examples in Europe, particularly in France;

b)   A more flexible solution involves not all members but only those interested in participating. This is the *Forschungsvereinigungen* system, which Spain could usefully investigate. Spain has, moreover, developed research associations in the past, though with very varying degrees of success;

c)   Solution *a* becomes more attractive when the government participates (e.g. up to 50 per cent, as often occurs in France) in the budget of the occupational centre. There are probably many instances in Spain to which this solution would seem applicable;

d)   Research effort on behalf of a particular branch of industry is co-ordinated by an organisation which centralises financial contributions, and arranges for the research to be conducted in any laboratory it considers suitable. This is a good solution provided the organisation or agency does in fact have access to laboratories capable of carrying out its orders. This of course applies to laboratories engaging in applied research, in close touch with industrial problems. In fact, Spain already has many such laboratories (the Central Electrotechnological Laboratory is a good example) but some need to be strengthened and probably some others have still to be established. The main thing is that such laboratories should be working from the industry standpoint, with constant concern for efficiency and able to make the transition to manufacturing and then marketing. This will be discussed further below. It is to be noted that the laboratories of the engineering training centres have a particularly important role here;

e) The above approach is very flexible and the commitment can be increased or decreased in accordance with needs. It is sometimes supplemented by automatic funding by the firms of a given branch in the form of a contribution to R & D; a case in point is OCIDE (Oficina de Coordinacion de Investigacion y Desarrollo Electrico – Electrical Research and Development Co-ordination Agency), established in 1983 and funded by a percentage (paid by the customer) added to electricity bills, and subsequently to coal bills as well. The amounts collected are substantial (some Ptas 2.5 billion) and may seem disproportionate to the CDTI budget.

Moreover, programme decisions go up to government level, whereas they ought to stem from the firms concerned. But this criticism must be qualified, because it seems that the concerted action is working well.

Recommendation No. 10   *The government's policy of opening public sector laboratories very widely to private sector contracts should be continued and developed.*

Recommendation No. 11   *Co-operative research funding via fixed contributions might create imbalances and discourage the firms concerned, so should be avoided as soon as incentives from the market itself are sufficient.*

VI. THE CENTRE FOR TECHNOLOGICAL AND INDUSTRIAL DEVELOPMENT (CDTI)

The essential instrument in MINER innovation policy, the CDTI has been operating along completely different lines since an Act of November 1983. Its essential features are:

- Its direction is in the hands of professional industrialists, not civil servants;
- Contracts with firms follow the ordinary rules for industrial contracts, avoiding the constraints of purely administrative rules;
- The CDTI operates not only through project-linked loans but also through equity participation, so that new firms can be set up (in 1984, 18 firms were established under the venture capital system);
- The CDTI tends to concentrate its efforts on "priority fields" which it has defined;
- Liaison with the Autonomous Communities is maintained via local innovation counsellors, who come under the Communities but are paid by the CDTI (this is discussed further in Chapter IX);
- Co-operation with the CAICYT has been considerably strengthened, especially through mutual representation, which has partly resolved the difficulties stemming from some slight degree of overlap in CDTI and CAICYT activities.

All these features are most valuable and provide the government with a particularly useful instrument for innovation.

Nevertheless the CDTI seems not to have had as much impact as might have been hoped on industrial development, even though it is remarkably quick at decision-making (six to eight weeks) and its policy is resolutely to encourage the smaller and medium-sized firm.

The reasons seem to be as follows:

- First, an inadequate budget (Ptas 2.657 million spent in 1984, and 4.658 million between 1977 and 1983);
- Then the relatively low number of projects adopted (less than one third); only some 300 projects received support between 1977 and 1984;
- Last, the lack of any financial incentive for projects, in the form of at least partial aid.

It is also possible that industry as a whole is not yet fully aware of the role the CDTI can play.

In view of its usefulness, and of the importance of the role it could play in Spain's technological development, the CDTI is the subject of the following recommendations:

Recommendation No. 12   *The CDTI, an essential instrument for the technological development of Spain, should be provided with a regularly growing budget over at least five to ten years.*

Recommendation No. 13   *The CDTI should be able to operate by providing partial or, in exceptional cases full grants, in addition to its customary working methods.*

Recommendation No. 14   *The research required for the various departments of the ministries should comprise a growing share of contract research in public and private sector industry laboratories. The CDTI should be responsible for managing such contracts.*

The above measures would be intended to accentuate the CDTI's own special character, distancing its role from that of a venture capital company. The financial yield to be expected from a CDTI operation should not be a major criterion but just one criterion among others.

Lastly, the CDTI should be concerned with the overall development of Spain's industrial fabric. While continuing its involvement with high technology sectors and with what is considered as priority fields, the CDTI should also support projects in small and medium-sized firms, *including those in traditional sectors* and even handicrafts. There are many examples of small firms in traditional sectors which need to assimilate new technologies in order to expand their growth: for example, the clothing sector can profitably use laser technology, the leather industry can produce collagen which is used in cosmetics or in contact lenses.

Criteria for the evaluation of the success of CDTI-led operations should not be exclusively scientific and technical. They must also take account of the realities affecting manufacture and commercialisation. Success, from this viewpoint, need not be manifest in more than a small number of cases (a "score" of 25 per cent would be excellent) and the CDTI should be judged more by the quality of its successes than by their numbers. Nevertheless, higher success rates may be expected with projects from smaller enterprises.

Recommendation No. 15   *The CDTI's sound policy in respect of SMEs should be pursued and developed, covering the more traditional sectors and even handicraft sectors. This implies a real effort in promotion, explanation and publicity.*

VII. OTHER MINISTRIES

Although the OECD Evaluation Group did not have an opportunity to examine the innovation resources and policies of other technological ministries in detail, the Group formed the opinion, perhaps wrongly, that most of these others are rather "poor relations" by comparison with the two major institutions discussed above. If that impression is accurate, it is to be feared that the other ministries may not have adequate resources at their disposal to develop innovations of their specific concern.

This seems, for example, to be the case of the Ministry of Agriculture. Although it possesses a coherent range of laboratories grouped together within Spanish Oceanographical Institute, its own agricultural and livestock laboratories do not seem to have been adequately developed. It is true that these are supplemented by numerous CSIC laboratories, but there is some doubt as to how far the policy of the Ministry of Agriculture can play its full role in them.

The point must again be made that applied research laboratories benefit from being directly placed under the authority of those requiring their results. Although the research contract mechanism – which should be retained and even strengthened – can correct this shortcoming to some extent, it can never do so completely.

The CSIC should confine itself to what is in any case the very wide field of basic research, and should transfer those of its laboratories covering science applications to agronomics and animal husbandry to a major National Institute for Agronomic Research.

The same applies, though probably to a lesser extent, to the Ministry of Health and Consumer Affairs. In the 1984 list of Spanish Public Research Centres, 13 centres are shown as coming under this ministry, to which must be added the considerable range of units under the National Health Institute. But among the latter it is difficult to ascertain which have really active and specialist research programmes. Most are simply shown with the rather uninformative mention *investigacion biomedica*.

But the CSIC has 34 centres engaged in both basic and applied research of direct interest to the Ministry of Health, which are however cut off from the life of its hospital centres.

The Ministry of Public Works, also, seems not to have an adequate research infrastructure at its disposal. As for the Eduardo Torroja Building and Cement Institute, which naturally is an applied research institute, this comes under the CSIC and its work seems neither recognised nor made use of.

There is little point in continuing this list, for which in any case the Group has only very sketchy information. On the other hand, two approaches may be suggested which should probably be followed simultaneously.

The first is to remodel the scientific and technological infrastructure. In some cases this is straightforward and should be put in hand at once. In other cases, particularly laboratories engaging both in basic and very applied research, detailed studies are needed, and their restructuring will inevitably be gradual.

The second solution is to strengthen the decision-making powers of the technological ministries in the research field, e.g. by creating a Research and Innovation Directorate where the ministry concerned does not have one. The Directorate would have control of the centres under their respective ministries, and responsibility for placing research contracts with outside agencies when necessary in order to implement research and innovation policies formulated and submitted to the Interministerial Commission.

A measure along these lines would facilitate the work of the Interministerial Commission, because all ministries would send it overall, summary and fully worked out dossiers.

Recommendation No. 16   *The innovation and research potential of the technological minis-tries should be strengthened, especially by restructuring and developing resources already available in Spain. Exploitation of this potential should be made the responsibility of a high authority within the ministry: for example a Director, or a high-level Scientific Counsellor, equipped with resources for investigation and programming.*

VIII. EMPLOYERS' ORGANISATIONS

Development of innovations within Spanish industry will essentially fall upon business leaders, who are likely to find themselves facing new problems. It will be indispensable to pool their thinking in order to solve these problems, and industrial leaders' associations (such as the Circulo de Empresarios) or their Federation (such as the Confederacion Espanola de Organizaciones Empresariales – CEOE) will have a decisive role to play in the years ahead.

There is no doubt that these organisations are fully aware of what is at stake, and their analysis of the situation is lucid and relevant.

It emphasizes the following points:

– R&D and innovation are being supported less in Spain than elsewhere;
– Foreign investment and accompanying technology transfers have probably reached their limits;
– The Spanish market shows a preference for foreign products;
– Foreign equipment is often preferred to Spanish equipment for government service contracts. This is at least partly due to the fact that foreign firms often offer products from a catalogue, with excellent descriptive literature and short delivery times, whereas some Spanish firms do not begin manufacture until they have an order – hence each job is "one off", involving long production delays.

Apart from these general comments, their analysis also draws attention to:

– Lack of co-ordination between the two ministries mainly responsible for developing innovation, the MEC and the MINER;
– The need for a central Spanish agency responsible for scientific and technological development policy;
– The CDTI's lack of flexibility in the past and the absence of grant-type incentives with which to intervene;
– The CSIC's lack of sufficient capacity to produce innovation matching the needs of Spanish industry.

Furthermore, business leaders fear that the Science and Technology Act[2] may emphasize the bureaucratic side of decision-making, and that the CDTI "priority" system, in which priorities are established without consultation with industry, may prejudice "ordinary" projects, which can take a wide variety of forms, in which industry is interested.

Most of these points are dealt with elsewhere in this report. Only those calling for action by industrial employers' associations will be examined here.

The actions of these associations should clearly result in effective concertation with government and public research agencies. Two recommendations are important here:

Recommendation No. 17   *It is desirable to ensure, as the new Bill provides, that industrial organisations be represented at the various levels of government responsible for scientific and technological policy. This point will be further examined in Chapter X.*

Recommendation No. 18   *The governing boards of the major national research institutes, such as the Boards of Directors and Scientific Committees, should include substantial representation from industry.*

Insufficient consultation shows up clearly in the minor but very revealing instance of the inventory of public research resources available for industry. The inventory exists, because it was published in 1984. But few industry leaders know about it and it is rather poorly tailored to their needs, since it gives no indication of the real potential of the agencies it lists: no information about staffing levels, major heavy equipment, overall volume of contracts, etc. Consultation when the inventory was being produced could have made it much more usable.

But there is one key factor in the new industrial policy which industry leaders and their associations seem not to have taken sufficiently into account. This report has already noted that industrial leaders want an improved public research infrastructure which can produce innovations that industry can buy, and which can also accept, e.g. under contract, to conduct the kind of research industry needs.

These industrial wishes are entirely reasonable, and the government should pay due regard to them. However, there seems to be some doubt as to how far industry leaders have realised that an essential precondition for commissioning work from an outside research institute and making profitable use of the results is to have in-house laboratory facilities of their own. As soon as possible (within five to ten years at most) the country's industrial research potential needs to be brought up to the European level. This will be a formidable undertaking, and while government support will often be essential, the brunt of the effort must be borne by the firms themselves.

Recommendation No. 19   *Industrial organisations, such as the CEOE, should set up a consultancy unit to help member firms develop in-house laboratories and to devise and implement programmes.*

Once industries have established a sound research and innovation capability of their own, they will be in a position to draw the best possible benefits from public research institutes and even from those of universities. The University-Industry Foundation will have a most important part to play.

Industry should also develop an ability to make informed decisions as to where co-operative research would be possible and desirable. There is at present some degree of scepticism in Spain about research associations, however the OCIDE and ASINEL are generally regarded as efficient.

Spanish industry has in fact yet to recognise the important role which research associations can play, not only in carrying out technical work but also in providing training for research management, in the analysis and distribution of information, and in international co-operation.

It is a fact that industry must become the driving force behind present and future research associations.

Recommendation No. 20   *Responsibility for arranging, devising and managing co-operative research programmes, when the need for these becomes evident, lies with the professional industrial organisations.*

Although the industrial organisations are favourable to the introduction of parafiscal levies, attention must be drawn to their unhelpful effects: unreliable matching of resources to needs, and a tendency to relieve industry of its responsibilities.

IX. PROBLEMS POSED BY DECENTRALISATION

Spain has wholeheartedly opted for decentralisation, which offers the great advantage of bringing the decision-maker closer to those who must live with the consequences, good or bad. But decentralisation also involves certain risks – national policy may lack coherence, and there may be scope for duplication of effort and waste.

It is true that decentralisation often results from sensitive political situations, or from deep, even passionate emotional reactions. The following discussion is based on the sole criterion of efficiency. This is not to underestimate the importance of other criteria, but to take these into account would be beyond what the OECD was asked to do. In any case, efficiency is a criterion which should never be lost from view.

In what now follows the terms "region" and "decentralisation" or "regionalisation" will be used to avoid prejudging the (probably evolving) legal status of the Provinces and Autonomous Communities. The analysis will therefore focus on what it would be logical to do – or arrange to have done – whether at central government or at regional levels. It will endeavour to identify and distinguish the various problems arising from the different kinds of research, development and support for innovation. From this, two fundamental concepts will emerge: the concept of *concertation* and the concept of *complementarity*, which will be discussed again by way of conclusion.

Basic research

This is carried out partly in the universities, and partly in the major research institutes. Universities are by nature decentralised, and academic staff should have very wide discretion as to the kind of research they engage in. Research adds to the stock of basic knowledge, thereby serving the national and, indeed, international scientific and technological community. But because such research is very free and discretionary in character, whether it is funded by central government or by the region has little significance. It is in fact preferable that a university should be closely associated with its own region, firstly because that is the most reliable way of involving it in regional activities (for which it can act as a centre of competence) and secondly because many regions have a need for basic local research, if only to explore their natural environments (the mouth of the river Ebro and the Guadalquivir basin raise different scientific questions; the Meseta and Galicia have different kinds of flora). Lastly, regional authorities can react rapidly to provide effective support for original scientific developments arising unexpectedly in a university department.

But, as has also been seen, a university can and should take part in systematic basic research efforts, programmed by a central agency such as was suggested in Chapter IV, Recommendation No. 4. That is to say that central government must be allowed a complementary role in the universities of the regions. This should not present difficulties.

Basic research is also conducted in major research establishments throughout Spain. This infrastructure, and the programmes being conducted within it, need to be co-ordinated if financial waste and loss of efficiency are to be avoided. A degree of centralisation is essential.

However, each region may wish to have the basic research it considers it requires conducted by, and within, local organisations. A region may even wish to establish a special institute to respond to its own fundamental preoccupations.

Here again, the solution appears to be simple. All that is required is for the region to be able to commission additional research projects in governmental institutes and, conversely, for government to be able to commission research in regional institutes where available.

The necessary co-ordination should be provided at the level of the institutes' governing bodies.

Recommendation No. 21   *The governing body of a leading research institute, regardless of which authority it comes under, should include representatives of national and regional institutions, capable of harmonizing the participation of these two types of authority.*

Applied research

The problems to be solved appear more difficult here, but they will be seen to be of the same nature as the foregoing, and to require similar solutions.

Applied research should clearly be carried out as close as possible to those who will be using the results. On the other hand, all applied research involves a substantial proportion of work of general interest. To list all possible instances would take a whole book: here it must suffice to discuss certain typical cases, and first of all the case of industrial research.

Industrial research is, or should be, carried out largely within firms themselves; these firms will often require assistance whether from government (via the MINER or the CDTI) from their own region (via agencies which in many cases have still to be established, see below) or from private bodies such as venture capital companies. Usually several different kinds of aid will be involved and will require concertation (see below, Chapter IX).

But it is to be noted immediately that the CDTI has already taken a very positive step in introducing innovation counsellors for the regions. Similarly, the emergence at regional level of such bodies as the CIDEM in Catalonia will ensure a unified concept of regional policy.

Good concerted action presupposes spokesmen in close contact with one another. The previous paragraph shows that this favourable combination can be achieved.

A second typical case is that of agronomic research, essential to Spain. It has been seen that the dispersal of resources between the Ministry of Agriculture and the Ministry of Education handicaps Spain, and that it would be desirable for the country to possess a single large-scale National Institute for Agronomic Research. This would raise the question of how to reconcile the existence of such a major national centre with the particular needs of the regions. The problem appears difficult, but experience has shown that simple solutions can be found.

A major institute of this nature in fact carries out both general research (applied genetics, plant pathology, etc.) and more specific kinds of research of interest to particular types of produce, and therefore to one or several regions.

It is therefore sensible for such an institute to have both central laboratories (generally organised by discipline though with interdisciplinary co-ordination) and also a network of decentralised laboratories associated with specific types of produce. The decentralised laboratories should maintain close links with the users of their results, but can also be of help in the general studies of the central laboratory, and may even be able to identify new lines of enquiry for it.

In practice, a decentralised laboratory requires a Scientific Committee which should include representatives of:

- The central laboratory;
- Regional authorities;
- Users in the region or regions interested in the research.

It will be important that Spain's research and innovation policy makers take account of the essential requirements stemming both from research necessities and actual needs.

A third typical case is that of public works. As with agronomic research, it would seem that the group of National Laboratories responsible for general research is not sufficiently developed. It needs strengthening and it needs to be given comprehensive and well-defined terms of reference.

But individual regions also require public sector research laboratories, in close touch with commissioning authorities and with contractors. France provides a typical example: besides the central Ponts et Chaussées Laboratory (the LCPC, which includes a number of units in the provinces) there is a network of Ponts et Chaussées laboratories (the LPCs) having programmes which depend on their region but which come under the scientific authority of the LCPC, whereby they are also involved in concerted research activities.

This system not only ensures decentralisation, but also the concertation of action and the circulation of information, together with unified technological design. The most important objective is to achieve good interaction between regional laboratories and the central unit.

Several other examples could be given. In fact, just a few very important recommendations may be suggested:

Recommendation No. 22 *The top-level body for the concertation of regional and national policies, should without delay set up a working group to devise criteria for funding the various kinds of research and support to innovation by central and regional government, and to work out the most appropriate arrangements for concerted action.*

Recommendation No. 23 *It will be in the interests of regions to provide themselves, as some have done already, with small research/innovation policy units equipped both for communication with central government agencies and also for defining ways and means of developing their regions.*

Recommendation No. 24 *Research institutes that are dependent on some major national research body (such as many CSIC laboratories) and located in the regions should invite representatives of the regions concerned to join their governing boards or science councils.*

Recommendation No. 25 *When several regions consider that each needs some similar kind of technological facility (e.g. test laboratory, public works laboratory, etc.) it will be advantageous to link these into a network and, in many cases, to set up a national laboratory to take charge of investigations of common interest and to act in an advisory capacity for the regional bodies.*

Many other recommendations could be suggested but they would all stem from two essential considerations:

- The need for effective consultation between central government and regions, by exchanging information and pooling ideas;
- The need for effective complementarity of projects, meaning that central government supports projects of general interest in the regions, while the regions support projects of value to them in government centres.

It is appropriate to conclude this Chapter by noting that many extremely interesting initiatives already exist, or are being established, in several regions:

- Industrial information systems such as that in Navarra;
- Close co-operation between university and industry, as in the Madrid region;
- Regional organisation for research co-ordination and support, as in Catalonia (CIRIT);
- Information agencies and enterprise development organisations, as in Catalonia (CIDEM).

The above list is illustrative only, and is clearly not exhaustive in any sense.

X. CO-ORDINATING THE NATIONAL EFFORT

As the Bill shows, Spain is well aware that co-ordination is an essential component of efficiency. The Bill[2] contains many invaluable elements which should be maintained at all costs. They are as follows:

a) The existence of a National Plan which promotes synthesis and coherency of the national effort in Science and Technology;

b) Recognition of the interministerial nature of scientific, technological and innovation issues;

c) The creation of the *Consejo Asesor para la Ciencia y la Tecnologia* (Advisory Council for Science and Technology) establishing a close liaison between the scientific community and those in charge of economic and social affairs;

d) The creation of the *Consejo General de la Ciencia y de la Tecnologia* (General Council for Science and Technology) to co-ordinate national with regional policies;

e) The provision of more effective status for certain leading research agencies;

f) The clear definition of the tasks for the *Comision Interministerial de la Ciencia y de la Tecnologia* (Interministerial Commission on Science and Technology);

g) An extended role for the CDTI.

The Bill does however attract to certain criticisms. The first, well expressed by the industrial organisations, is its essentially administrative and juridical nature, raising fears of stultifying red tape. If the system is to function properly it is essential that:

– The Commission be assisted by an adequately staffed secretariat to carry out studies, prepare proposals and draft decisions;

– That the overall development and innovation policy be orchestrated by a high level individual, exclusively dedicated to this assignment with authority extending to the co-ordination accross ministries.

The setting up of the secretariat will necessarily follow, though problems could arise over how it should be financed. It would therefore be preferable to provide for this from the outset.

As for the distinguished and highly-placed leader, this person will rapidly become indispensable, since the work of a committee (and in this instance, a collection of committees) cannot go beyond two albeit very important tasks:

– To confront varying and sometimes strikingly different points of view;

– To formulate options and take decisions on the basis of carefully studied proposals.

The assessments of viewpoints should be based on detailed analyses of the problems to be resolved, and on studies conducted under the authority of a distinguished personality having direct contact with the realities and people involved in scientific, technological and innovative development.

There are many possible ways of doing this. The best would probably be to establish a post of Special Science Adviser to the Government who would also run the secretariat for which the need has already been noted. In the eyes of public opinion this person would embody modern Spain's determination and vigour in scientific and technological innovation, in the same way as does the United States "Science Adviser to the President", at the head of certain White House services.

Another solution would be to have the Interministerial Commission chaired by a Minister in charge of the Commission secretariat and councils *but with no other portfolio.* This was the French solution as of 1985, which worked well, above all probably because of the exceptional capabilities of the incumbent, Mr. Hubert Curien. This solution is adopted, in part, by the Spanish Bill which provides that, in the transition period, the interministerial Commission be chaired by the Minister of Education.

One might even imagine the Interministerial Commission being placed directly under the Prime Minister. Spain is hardly ready to adopt so radical a solution – which is perhaps to be regretted.

Recommendation No. 26   *Responsibility for formulating scientific and technological develop-*
ment policies should be in the hands of some distinguished person,
acting as leader for all preparatory studies and work of the
Interministerial Commission, the Advisory Council and the General
Council. The person should be given a title reflecting Spain's
commitment to development;

Another deficiency in the Bill relates to the infrastructure for conducting research. This needs to be developed. A certain amount of regrouping and co-ordination will be essential. Most of all, the research potential of certain technological ministries needs considerable strengthening. The Bill itself should certainly not enter into the detail of measures to be taken, but it should include the development and rationalisation of Spain's scientific and technological infrastructure among the tasks of the Interministerial Commission.

Recommendation No. 27   *A paragraph should be added to the text of the Bill in the section*
dealing with the tasks of the Interministerial Commission, con-
cerning the key part the Commission should play in developing and
rationalising the executive infrastructure of scientific and techno-
logical research.

One of the many interesting points in the Bill is an innovation regarding the legal status of certain leading research institutions. But in fact all research laboratories, large or small, and especially those engaged in applied or technological research, need a special status to facilitate management and foster outward-looking attitudes.

Recommendation No. 28   *The text of the Bill should provide for a suitable status not only for*
leading research establishments but also, perhaps under different
forms, for small and medium-sized research institutes which, like
the largest, should each have a governing body and a science
committee.

XI. APPEALING TO PUBLIC OPINION (PSYCHOLOGICAL APPROACHES)

Psychological approach is essential and everyone involved in research and development share these sentiments. The country as a whole needs to feel involved in its scientific and technological commitment, and to understand that although technology can be bought in, Spain can only buy it wisely and economically if she is herself able to produce it, as a member of the world group of countries creating progress. This is a major prerequisite for economic independence.

A public information campaign is needed to explain the issues. This should be provided for not only in central government policy but also in the regions, as well as by leading personalities in economics, industrial associations, chambers of commerce, etc.

The campaign should make use of all media – posters, press, radio and television. The success of the recently broadcast television programmes on science is particularly encouraging. Such programmes should be systematically designed and transmitted, and should find an important place not only in scientific research but in technical, industrial and agronomic activities, etc., so that public opinion should be aware that Spain has her own specific national development programmes.

But the campaign should also make use of specific events and operations such as, for example:

a) Every industrial or technological trade fair (e.g. Expo Quimia in Barcelona) where the Government should have a stand at which to describe the broad lines and reasons for its policy;

b) Mobile exhibitions (and, perhaps, a Technology Centre) which need to be designed and assembled quickly;

c) Clubs for the initiation of young people into technology (aerospace, informatics, computers, history of discoveries, etc.) which should be set up by educational establishments and, perhaps, by public sector laboratories which might establish "associations for young friends of the laboratories";

d) "Open days", which should be arranged every year by the leading public and private sector research institutes.

Public opinion might be even more impressed by the creation of a substantial Royal Award for Spanish Technological Progress to be formally conferred every year by the King himself.

Many other activities could be envisaged. Suffice it here to make one very general recommendation, leaving the field free to the imagination of all concerned in advancing innovation in Spain.

Recommendation No. 29   *Public opinion should be persuaded by all possible means of the need for a commitment alike to basic and to applied research in the interests of Spain's future economic competitiveness.*

XII. INNOVATION POLICY OR RESEARCH POLICY

The preceding chapters cover all aspects of Spanish policy that the authorities considered it necessary to communicate to the OECD's Evaluation Group, the members of which were much impressed by the dynamic character of this new policy. However, the policy at present seems to be one for the development of scientific and technical research rather than for the development of innovation. And although it is true that a good R&D programme often (though not always) makes an essential contribution to innovation, this alone is not sufficient.

It is therefore necessary – and this is the object of the present Chapter – to pick out, from among the various measures taken, those which typically relate to innovation policies, at the same time noting some gaps and deficiencies which it would be desirable to correct.

In order to clarify the problems posed by innovation policies, it is useful to distinguish three types of innovation:

  a) Those which do not involve advanced scientific knowledge, but simply require good technological know-how and a keen appreciation of clients' needs. Their development consists in trials, measurements, tests, a good method of value analysis and, in due course, a rigorous organisation of industrial production;

  b) Those which involve substantial existing scientific knowledge without requiring any further extension of knowledge. Laying on applied research, they often require laboratory work, and above all pilot or semi-industrial installations;

  c) Those calling for an extension of knowledge beyond that which already exists. This is the case with most advanced technological innovations, in which scientific and technological researches go hand-in-hand.

The measures analysed earlier in this report appear for the most part likely to benefit and facilitate this last type of innovation. Even the CDTI, which is equipped to assist all innovations, is likely – due to its defined priorities – to favour type *c* more than the others. However, commercial and export successes are most frequently achieved by innovations of types *a* or *b*.

Spain has achieved a number of successes in these domains. Here are some examples:

  – Spain has made important advances, from the bases of American processes, in re-constituted woods (MDF or medium density fibers) which can be perfectly turned, carved or chiselled, or otherwise worked, and which have a very pleasant appearance; these products have acquired considerable importance since the country entered the Common Market. They represent innovation of type *b* in the USA where they originated, and of type *a* in Spain;

  – Spain is an important exporter of ceramics, including many innovative products of type *b*.

85

Measures contributing to the development of innovation in Spain, but which are clearly distinct from those expected to increase scientific and technical research potential, include the following:

- Opening public laboratories to contracts for private industry;
- The strengthening of the CDTI;
- Encouraging its decentralisation.

The preceding chapters have indicated various deficiencies in these measures; for example the CDTI needs to develop a formula for rewarding success (both industrial and commercial); likewise an infrastructure for technical control and testing; more generally, the technical research infrastructure still leaves much to be desired.

However, other elements exist in Spain which favour innovation although they have not resulted from any particular measures: they are nonetheless welcome. Examples are:

- The existence of research associations, set up on the initiative of the CAICYT, of which some (such as ASINEL in the electrical industry) are very active while others seem to vegetate: an overall policy of support and activation for these associations would seem to be called for;
- The existence of mutual guarantee companies (SGRs) with legal frameworks as fixed in 1978, which enable SMEs (small and medium enterprises) to take calculated risks;
- The existence of complementary systems (probably too complex) designed to facilitate the operation of SGRs, the Second Guarantee mixed Company, refinancing companies such as SOGASA (subsidiary guarantee company). It may also be recalled that the SGRs belong to their own confederation, the CESGAR. Thus Spain has a very interesting system for protecting and safeguarding SMEs, a system which will repay study and which might well be copied in other countries, provided they could avoid its complexity;
- The existence of IMPI which includes among its functions the promotion of SGRs, in some of which it may participate as protecting partner (socio protector); IMPI likewise participates in the complementary systems cited above;
- The existence of venture capital companies, along the lines of one originally created in Spain in 1976, on the initiative of the Bank of Bilbao, with numerous industrial and institutional partners even including the World Bank. This example has been widely followed: by the *Fomento de Inversiones Industriales* (industrial investment support), by the *Sociedad Bancaya de Promocion Empresarial* (venture capital), by the *Empresa Nacional de Innovacion* (ENISA – national innovation company created by the INI), and by many *Sociedades de Desarrollo Industrial* (SODIS – industrial development companies) having more or less regional interests. There are those who believe that venture capital companies cannot be justified and should be made part of the normal banking system. In fact the two are better separated, firstly because venture capital operations require novel decision procedures (based on future potential rather than results over the past five years), and secondly because each venture capital shareholder is kept fully informed of the activities being supported by his money.

Although it is true that the policy currently being followed in Spain is essentially one of scientific and technical research, it would be wrong to deny that there is also a policy of innovation. Spain's problem is thus basically that of encouraging the fullest use of these elements. But there is also a need to improve the elements as they exist; the criticisms set out in the preceding chapters have shown that it would be relatively easy to overcome their deficiencies. Lastly, certain missing elements need to be added in order to complete the system. In the following paragraphs some of these elements are suggested.

A first missing (or at least insufficiently developed) element is found in training, both for youth and for entrepreneurial management.

Concerning youth, the Evaluation Group regretted that lack of time prevented them from making a detailed study of education and training – whether at elementary of higher levels – designed to foster creativity and ability to innovate.

It would be valuable to compare the Spanish budget for practical work with that of other countries. Data in this field seem not to exist, which is most unfortunate since such data can provide a reasonably accurate and quantifiable indication of a country's potential for innovation. In any case, as has already been noted, it would seem that Spain is not very well placed in this field, although valuable efforts have been made since the early 1970s to reorganise the Spanish education system. But it should be recognised, however, that at the very beginning of the 1970s tremendous work had to be undertaken in order to raise school attendance up to the European level. Since the restoration of democracy, government has endeavoured, in accordance with the 1978 Constitution, to organise free and compulsory basic education for children between four and fourteen years of age. As the Spanish Authorities themselves stated, teaching programmes have changed very little whereas technical teaching programmes have not been expanded enough. The secondary education reform, currently under way, is likely to improve the situation to provide new features to support an efficient innovation policy. Now that the public education sector is rather well established, the State can fully play its role for the promotion of new generations of innovative technicians and entrepreneurial managers.

Concerning entrepreneurial managers, there are in Spain consulting firms which organise training seminars. But these seem to be principally devoted to improving management skills and, by comparison, innovation strategies receive very little attention. It is likely that these firms will develop; if not it will be necessary for government – and above all regional – authorities to consider intervention by creating appropriate *ad hoc* bodies. The Examiners were very pleased by the initiative of the IESE (Instituto de Estudios Superiores de la Empresa – Enterprise Institute of Higher Education) and the Public Enterprise Foundation to develop a training programme (INTE) for entrepreneurs for the management of R&D and its integration in the firms' strategy.

In any case, it is incumbent on these authorities to establish within the higher education system, special training courses on technological innovation of the type which already exist in France in some chairs of economics, such as in the Conservatoire National des Arts et Métiers. These training courses, which are intended not only for students but also for engineers and managers, are aimed at developing knowledge of the complex system of mechanisms and strategies of innovation.

A second missing element is an infrastructure to help innovating – and very often young – entrepreneurs. The prescription is simple and there is no lack of examples; the Berlin Land has undertaken such an action – an excellent model to copy – in promoting the creation of a "Technology and Innovation Park". A large (30 000 m^2) disused factory has been rented by Berlin's Technical University to accommodate specially-created research units in novel fields; the resulting creative environment is extremely dynamic.

Young enterprises in advanced technology are welcomed into this environment with very favourable financial conditions, and are helped with advice and information. The fact that this "Park" of advanced technological research brings together, under the same roof, both well-established undertakings and new ones which are sometimes still at project stage, has proved of extreme value. The "Park" is, in fact, an incubator for innovative enterprises.

This example certainly merits reflection. Its creation resulted not from a legislative text, but simply from local public and private initiatives; demonstrating that innovation policy in large measure consists in creating the right "spirit", often combined with practical example. This is not the place to develop further all the various possibilities, but one typical example may be cited. The Spanish *Plan for Informatics* envisages the establishment of a research institute: this certainly appears a wise proposal, but its impact would be enormously greater if it were combined with an "enterprise maternity clinic" similar to that of the Berlin Land.

Another deficiency is the tendency to use the Spanish State market as pacemaker for production when, as noted previously, that customer would rather buy through catalogues which can sometimes lead to foreign purchases being preferred. This clearly highlights the frequently observed conflict between short-term imperatives and longer-term idealism. In the Spanish State market sufficient advance notice needs to be given to allow time for an innovative national product to be born and satisfactorily produced. There is no need to look around for an example of this: a very good one is to be found in Spain, in the operating methods of *La Telefonica* which should be a lesson for all administrative bodies even if it be objected that the firm has a private character (the State has only a minority holding, although the company has a monopoly) as well as a network of undertakings on which, through its participation, it can have direct influence. In fact the main difference distinguishing *La Telefonica* from certain other administrations is that it has developed and adopted a long-term strategy.

However, as was said earlier, the real essential is to know how to make use of every available element. There are two such elements which can play a determinant role: the enterprises themselves, and the regional administrations. The enterprises have been examined already, it being concluded that their mentality must embrace development and innovation. As has been recognised by the *Circulo de Empresarios* (contractors'club) Spanish entry into the Common Market – will help towards recognition of the changes so often necessary.

It will be useful here to give special attention to the role of regional authorities. It seems clear that a centralised co-ordination of research is necessary: this is demonstrated by the NSF in the USA and by the DFG in Germany. On the other hand, there is no doubt that innovation can benefit from decentralisation.

Help for innovation in fact supposes information transfers (often of great variety), evaluation of ideas and of men, creation of financial structures (often of original nature), and very close liaisons between all concerned with innovation policy and with the innovator himself – manifest or potential. It is natural and at the same time necessary that ANVAR (Agence nationale pour la valorisation de la recherche) in France, like the CDTI in Spain, be decentralised: it is also natural and necessary that regional authorities should set up in their own areas the various mechanisms needed for the development of innovation.

It is the task of regional authorities to ensure that national mechanisms are used to the full by local innovators, but it is also – and above all – necessary that they develop in their own regions specific mechanisms such as mutual guarantee companies, venture capital companies (second guarantee systems being better situated at national level), technology and innovation "parks", training systems for innovation management, information systems specially concerned with markets rather than with legal, fiscal and legislative texts or technological data.

The Evaluation Group was above all able to learn about, and measure, the effort devoted by Spain to policies for scientific and technical development. That effort is easier to understand than the policies of innovation as such – of which scientific and technical development are no more than a component, albeit an essential one. For, despite efforts to decentralise, scientific and technical policies still remain largely centralised, with regional actions generally playing complementary roles in overcoming deficiencies and strengthening further strong points.

On the other hand many elements of an innovation policy, by their very nature, call for decentralisation, which incidentally accounts for the difficulty of evaluating such a policy, which cannot be fairly or completely judged through reports, but only *in situ*.

That being said, the Evaluation Group formed a very favourable opinion of Spain's regional efforts, based on what they saw in Catalonia and Asturias, and what they learnt about Navarra and the region of Valencia.

The mechanism seen in Catalonia, although oriented more towards research than towards innovation, should nonetheless prove most effective in support of the latter. Catalonia is also making a very substantial effort to increase the awareness of young people and prepare them for both research and innovation.

In Navarra, an important effort has been undertaken to ensure that innovators know where laboratories exist which can help them. In Valencia a dynamic and creative Design Centre has been established.

So also in Asturias the experts had the opportunity to get a sense of the level of efforts being prompted by the local government and its Ministry for Industry to revitalise industry in this region particularly affected by the crisis in steel and shipbuilding industries. Some of the more interesting initiatives are: the development under the leadership of a dynamic team of young professors of improved industry-university relations, the setting-up of a local venture-capital company and the creation of an industry and science park designed to offer advantageous conditions for establishment to new-born firms, possibly including foreign firms subsidiaries.

It should be noted, however, that this type of science park does not operate as an "incubator" for new firms which would possess such essential features as providing the firms with housing, common services and help for development. The incubator concept is considered to be one of the more efficient and cheaper solutions, the interest of which has been underlined earlier in this report.

These initiatives are receiving full support from central government, be it from the Department in charge of Innovation Policy at the Ministry of Industry, or from the CDTI whose local representative has very close links with the scientific and industrial leaders who participate in a regional "circle".

This regional innovation policy, though still in an embryonic state, should bear fruit in the long run, if the professionalism and enthusiasm currently observed are preserved.

But there remains a problem. Certain areas are considered in priority and benefit from much planning effort, the country's *Plan for Informatics* being a good example. These plans should cover every aspect of innovation, from fundamental research to the opening up of markets. It is to be feared that the plans do not succeed in making sufficient appeal to regional dynamisms, nor in correctly distinguishing between what should be centralised and dependent on high authority, and what should be largely decentralised and so attract –and co-ordinate – the maximum of local initiatives.

Finally, it will be noticed that two subjects have been omitted from this evaluation, standardization and patents. Spain's entry into the European Community will in fact result in important changes in these areas, and it is too early to know how the country will react to the ensuing new opportunities and new constraints.

XIII. CONCLUSION

The present study has endeavoured to draw attention to some of the risks confronting Spain's new science and technology development policy. For this reason it stresses gaps and deficiencies in that policy, which will probably be quickly filled by the new structures and authorities soon to be introduced. Meanwhile it is possible that the study may give an erroneous impression of being exclusively critical.

Its readers and users are therefore urged to see it in its overall context, and to bear in mind two essential conclusions.

The first is that none of the measures already taken or contemplated is criticised. Attention is drawn to some gaps in the policy, but no major defect has been identified.

The second is that Spain's dynamism is real and genuine, Spanish laboratories having already achieved some outstanding results even without the support of a national policy. Some of the laboratories concerned are renowned abroad, where sometimes they are better known and appreciated than at home.

The great problem for the new policy of innovation in Spain, as in many other countries, is to free good initiatives from restriction, help them to flourish and co-ordinate them for maximum efficiency, without stifling them by burdening bureaucratic decisions too remote from the realities of research and innovation. For this, it is particularly necessary to make the fullest use of all the advantages offered by regionalisation, rather than suffering it.

NOTES AND REFERENCES

1. The Bill, enacted the 14th April 1986, contains a clause (disposicion adicional No. 1) which stipulates that within six months of the Law coming into force, the CAYCIT be abolished and that its personnel and equipment be transferred to the Permanent Commission, the structure of which is to be defined by the Government.

2. During the Examiners' stay in Spain in May 1985, they were given the text of a Draft Bill on Science, Technology and Innovation. Throughout this Report, we refer to this particular text, and the Examiners' recommendations are based on that text. Since then some amendments were introduced in the Bill before it was enacted in April 1986, therefore some of the recommendations became obsolete.

Part III

ACCOUNT OF THE REVIEW MEETING

I. INTRODUCTION

The Committee for Scientific and Technological Policy reviewed this report on 1st December 1986 in Madrid. It was chaired by Mrs. Kerstin Eliasson, Vice-Chairman of the Committee (Sweden) and took place in the presence of the three Examiners and a high level Spanish delegation led by Mr. L.C. Croissier, Minister of Industry and Energy (MINER), and Mr. J.M. Maravall, Minister of Education and Science (MEC).

The session was opened by *Mr. Marcum*, Director for Science, Technology and Industry at the OECD. Mr. Marcum, referring to the procedure adopted for this series of reviews of innovation policies of Member countries following the reviews of science and technology policies carried out since 1963 by the OECD, stressed the interest shown in this type of analysis in France, Australia (which had used it in defining its own new policy) and Sweden (whose Prime Minister had taken a personal interest in the review).

The basic principles of Spain's new science, technology and innovation policy were successively described by *Mr. Croissier*, Minister of Industry and Energy, and *Mr. Maravall*, Minister of Education and Science.

Mr. Croissier, after thanking the OECD for the work it had done, pointed out that not long ago it would have been impossible to speak of innovation policy in Spain, since none had existed until very recently. Technology used to be purchased and very little was done to develop specifically Spanish techniques. Spain's entry into the Common Market had meant that awareness of the need to innovate and be competitive both in price and quality was now growing even more rapidly.

The Spanish Government had launched a vast campaign to improve the country's performance through:

– Adoption of the Science and Technology Act;
– Deployment of very effective action by the CDTI; and
– International co-operation (Spain would be chairing EUREKA in 1987).

On the first point, the Minister pointed out that the Act was not an isolated measure: other legislation on patents, trademarks, standardization and type approval had been enacted or was being prepared.

The policy of the CDTI was to help firms participate in innovation with an element of risk, through a system of loans excluding subsidies. In 1985, more than 30 per cent of its budget had come from returns on earlier operations. As CDTI activity was stepped up, aid for INI industrial restructuring had been scaled down.

In the case of international co-operation, 14 Spanish projects had already been approved by EUREKA. (At the time when this report was drafted, 21 projects had been approved.)

The Minister also stressed the rise in government spending on R&D (up 57 per cent) but added that it was essential that industry also make an R&D effort. Moreover, technological innovation was not the only consideration. Better design and more agressive marketing were also needed.

Mr. Maravall, Minister of Education and Science, explained why a large-scale science and technology policy had been delayed in Spain: a paradoxically liberal but protectively autarkic regime had resulted in the importation of foreign technologies with little domestic development, leading to a spontaneous type of R&D system with practically no co-ordination, impetus or guidance, supported by very limited human resources.

In demonstrating the interdependence between scientific and economic development, the OECD had shown the way which Spain had now taken in adopting a global policy to revive research, development, innovation and the economy as a whole by co-ordinating the action of ten ministries. Thus, the Act on the development and general co-ordination of scientific and technical research, important as it was in itself, took on its full meaning only when seen as part of a whole body of legislation on the universities, industry, patents, standardization, etc.

The Minister then went into the details of the first-mentioned Act, with its concepts of National Plan and co-ordination. The instrument of this co-ordination was the Interministerial Commission, together with the General Council for Science and Technology, in which the autonomous communities participated and the Evaluation Council, chaired by the Minister of Industry and Energy, which function is to coordinate with the private sector, the enterprises and the unions.

The National Plan would include all the priorities already defined and, in addition, some horizontal initiatives of very broad scope, in particular:

– A programme for training researchers in Science and Technology; and
– A programme for scientific information and documentation.

Special attention would be paid to the R&D infrastructure: a new status for the major national agencies, creation of institutes of micro-electronics, biotechnology, etc.

Thus, Spain had graduated from a spontaneous model in an autarkic system – which was stifling R&D – to one that was both co-ordinated and concerted.

The Minister ended by saying that the new system was essentially "open". While the possibility of appointing a Minister of Research had not been ruled out, Spain preferred, at least for the moment, a flexible and co-ordinated system within which individual responsibilities could develop.

The machinery thus set up would be used to draw up the National Plan, for approval by the government around April 1987. It was remarkable that Spain had been able to set this reorganisation afoot as it entered the Common Market.

The Chairman, *Mrs. Eliasson*, stressed that the OECD reviews were of interest not only for the country under study, but also for all the other Member countries, since they were a means of passing on experience. In this regard, the general discussion of the methods and results of the reviews at the OECD workshop held in Paris in June 1986 had been very useful.

Speaking for the Examiners, *Mr. Piganiol* referred to the difficulties of evaluating an innovation support policy: it lay somewhere between an R&D policy and an industrial policy, and its specific features should be hidden by the interaction between the two. Furthermore, the review of Spain had taken place at a time of reform in every area with, however, a remarkable attention to coherence and global coverage. Since the reforms, a number of the Examiners' recommendations were now out of date. The long interval between the evaluation itself and the present review meeting meant that the latter had both to discuss an Examiners' Report and recommendations in the usual way and at the same time update many points in a study that had been produced in the midst of change. The Examiners had been struck by the dynamics of this change, supported by a strong political will and guided with remarkably clear-sighted objectivity.

The review of Spain – one of the very first carried out by the OECD on Member countries' innovation policies – could not therefore be a generally applicable prototype: it was set apart in that it had to consider industrial and R & D policies as a whole as well as innovation policy, and not only with respect to past achievements but to the future too. That made the present exercise particularly interesting, and it had only been possible because of the co-operation and openness of the Spanish authorities, to whom the Examiners wished to extend their warmest thanks. Their frankness and willingness to co-operate had made it easier to draft a report which would otherwise have been difficult to write, since it concerned not a static but a constantly changing situation that was in many respects quite remarkable.

II. REFORM OF THE SCIENCE AND TECHNOLOGY SYSTEM

This topic was introduced by *Mr.Huberman* after *Mr. Bell*, Head of the OECD Science and Technology Policy Division, had recalled the procedure adopted by the OECD for the evaluation studies.

Mr. Huberman noted that the review had taken place while the Act was being framed. This Act was an extremely positive factor for the future of Spain, since it created a framework and mechanism for consultation with a view to the development of innovation. Moreover, a good balance had been struck between the need for a coherent and therefore centralised policy and at the same time more contacts with local and regional bodies, so that researchers and those who use their findings could co-operate more closely. The National Plan procedure, which involved an annual report to Parliament, was also very satisfactory.

But Mr. Huberman emphasized that the establishment of this framework for action was only the beginning, not the end, of a process by which an innovation policy is developed. While that beginning was remarkable, he believed that the points which could be criticised should be considered, rather than dwelling on the qualities of the decisions that had been taken. He felt that the Bill relied too heavily on only two ministries. The action of others must also be stepped up, and co-ordination between all agencies maintained.

Furthermore, the structure proposed involved many committees and did not include a full-time director who would instigate and follow up operations. Mr. Huberman was not arguing in favour of a Ministry of Science and Technology, since the idea was to co-ordinate the action of all the ministries involved. But the efficient operation of the agencies set up called for a permanent organiser with extensive powers. This was in any case necessary to prevent the system being bogged down in bureaucracy.

Mr. Huberman then voiced his concern as to the development of innovation in Spain and referred to the analysis of the types of innovation described in Chapter XII of the Background Report. The CDTI effectively corresponded to type c innovations, which called for an extension of scientific and technological knowledge. But innovations with little or no scientific content did not enjoy the same support, although they were just as essential to competitiveness. A testing, research and advisory infrastructure must be created and, above all, Spain must value innovation at home at its true worth. Attitudes must be changed, including those of the financial institutions, which were more concerned with commercial operations than industrial ventures. The days when Spain could simply buy technology abroad were over.

After thanking the Examiners and the OECD Secretariat, *Mr. Rojo*, Secretary of State for the Universities and Research, pointed out that many of the Examiners' criticisms and recommendations no longer applied, since they had been taken into account in the rapid adaptation of the Spanish institutional framework. The report ought therefore to be updated.

The legislation created a general framework for consultation and co-ordination, while avoiding cumbersome bureaucracy. This framework was also flexible and allowed adjustment. In addition, provision was made for the National Plan to be reviewed annually and submitted to Parliament.

Why had this flexible model been chosen in preference to some other, such as a ministry or authority linked with the President? The reason was that the government felt that consultation and co-ordination were urgent. The first problem to be solved concerned co-operation between industry and the universities; the latter had in the past concentrated on teaching but had now begun to expand their research and ought therefore to be included in scientific and technological development policy.

Legislation had also to allow for the existence of the autonomous communities. Here again, flexibility was necessary to ensure maximum synergy at regional level while maintaining that central co-ordination without which the various National Plan operations would not attain the critical threshold of effectiveness. The CSIC had also conducted a remarkable policy of liaison with the "Autonomias", signing eleven outline agreements with them (the same applied to the INRA).

In passing, Mr. Rojo stressed the importance of evaluating programmes and research. This was essential not only for the efficient application of Spanish policy, but also for the purposes of liaison with research in other European countries.

There could be no real progress without an improvement in the quality of life; hence the importance attached to the human sciences, which would not be neglected.

The innovation process was very complex. Industrial competition must be encouraged and the innovative role of the SMEs developed, notably by seeing that they had access to skilled personnel. This implied more university training. Then there was the time factor. In stepping up the research effort in Spain, capacity to absorb the financial aid provided must be taken into account. The proportion of GNP earmarked for research had been increased from 0.37 per cent in 1982 to 0.65 per cent in 1985. Mr. Rojo attached great importance to an "operational approach" covering every stage, including lead times for training personnel; that stage was probably the most important, but it was certainly not the only one. Medium and long-term planning was necessary. The shortage of electronics and telecommunications skills was due to inadequate planning.

Stressing that the expansion of university research must go hand in hand with industrial development, Mr. Rojo mentioned CDTI grants and start-up aid for technological development projects and specific joint ventures. Aid was sometimes international. He quoted one project (AVENO) which involved five firms in three countries, two universities and three hospital research centres, total funding amounting to some Ptas 1 billion.

The 1983 university reform Act had established R&D as inseparable from higher education, and was revolutionary in that an academic career now depended not, as in the past, on competitive examinations of candidates' knowledge but on assessment of actual achievement. The policy was to promote university R&D and raise researchers' status so that the university was no longer, as in the past, an ivory tower. Substantial royal awards for meritorious work in the arts, the exact sciences and technology had been created and were conferred on winners by the King himself.

Policy thus aimed at quality and diversification, but also at economic relevance, by setting clear priorities. Programmes were assessed before, during and after their performance. Evaluation of the quality of results, whether *ex ante*, *interim* or *ex post*, was not always easy, and OECD experience would be valuable, since appraisal of research and technological innovation was a very delicate matter.

Mr. Huberman approved the intentions underlying the organisational model chosen, which should be retained, at least for the moment.

Mr. Piganiol noted that the Examiners had regretted that the Bill stipulated no budgetary commitment. In Spain this was not in fact possible, since such appropriations could be made only under the Finance Act. The Act did, however, provide for a credit line specifically for scientific and technological development (section IV, in fine), and this was of great importance.

Mr. Larsson (Sweden) described his own country's science policy co-ordinating agency and pointed out that the new Bill aimed to increase co-ordination, with closer involvement of the twelve ministers concerned.

Mr. Denozios (Greece) alluded to the time factor mentioned by Mr. Rojo. Co-ordination must take account of that factor and avoid being influenced by pressure groups with short-term objectives. Responsibility for scientific and technological development policy must be in the hands of a full-time director with extensive powers and the authority to override, if necessary, the various ministers concerned.

Mr. Paillon (EEC) agreed that responsibility should be in the hands of a strong authority. He stressed that programming and evaluation were intimately related, and noted that efficient dissemination of information was a prerequisite for efficient co-ordination. How was this organised? What data banks were used?

Mrs. Solanes (OECD Secretariat)) said that the OECD had completed a report on evaluation methods; a report to be published in 1987 would deal mainly with university research. The OECD was also studying methods of evaluating research personnel needs. Mrs. Solanes had noted Mr. Rojo statement concerning the fact that economic relevance criteria (or "opportunity criteria") were to be considered; but in that case, how was the proportion of free investigatory research to be determined?

In his reply, *Mr. Rojo* pointed out that the policy and operational levels must not be confused. Policy was the responsibility of the Interministerial Commission, while at the operational level it was the General Secretariat that was responsible.

The Act implied a moral commitment to increase the R&D budget that had in fact been honoured, since that budget was 37 per cent higher in 1986 than in 1985. Moreover, the university budget had been increased by 25 per cent and the combined CDTI-CSIC budget doubled.

Mr. Rojo thanked the OECD for the promise of help with evaluation. The time factor was very important, and it was quite true that ministries tended to concentrate on the short term – hence the interest of the National Plan, which provided for rolling five-year budgetary planning with annual updating.

Lastly, the National Plan included both vertical programmes (computers, environment, new technologies, etc.) and horizontal programmes (training, information, etc.). Mr. Rojo said he personally attached a great deal of importance to the general progress of knowledge, which would provide a host of new ideas for applied research and contribute to training researchers in all fields.

Here quality criteria were patently more important than opportunity criteria.

It was now beginning to be possible to measure the increase in the Spanish contribution to the international production of knowledge – 23 per cent in chemistry, 55 per cent in biology and 20 per cent in physics – though it had to be admitted that the starting level had been very low.

III. MOBILISATION OF THE INDUSTRIAL SECTOR: TECHNOLOGY ASSIMILATION AND PRODUCTION

This topic was introduced by *Mr. Ratz*, who said it was important for the Examiners to know the attitude of Spanish industry and society to R&D and to innovation problems. Certainly, in the past, the Spanish market had shown a preference for imported products – so why bother to innovate? Furthermore, Spanish industry had found it difficult to offer complete off-the-shelf packages in response to government invitations to tender.

But these were problems of the past. In the same way, many industries in Spain's large nationalised sector (INI) were in difficulties, and restructuring grants to those industries had been cut back sharply so that R&D effort could be boosted and new enterprises, especially SMEs, promoted. This was a highly important change of policy.

Free marketeers were in principle hostile to direct subsidies for industry and preferred tax incentives. But these often did not only apply to the recipient industries (such as in the case of Austria). The role of Government was not only to give an impetus to R&D. It was itself a market (El estado es impulsador y comprador), and that market had its part to play in development policy. In any case, the Government did not only buy capital goods. It could buy research from firms, as in the United States, and that was by far preferable to granting subsidies. In fact, Spain had the means to implement a complex and efficient policy. For example, to produce locomotives of a new design, the CDTI could, after putting out the tender, fund the prototype, while the Government guaranteed the subsequent purchase of a series (from which the CDTI would recover its costs).

As the innovative capacity of the universities and public research establishments increased, firms must be kept fully informed of the research and innovation possibilities available. Information alone, however, was not enough. Aid and advisory services must be installed at the interface between research and industry, since without them there would always be a lack of communication between the universities and the SMEs whose co-operation was so essential.

Apart from one or two notable exceptions, co-operative research was not particularly effective in Spain. Industry-linked centres should be funded by compulsory contributions supplemented by voluntary contributions (sometimes for specific purposes). But it was idle to believe that such centres could be fully financed by the industry concerned; the actual proportion of their budget covered was 50-60 per cent, so a government subsidy was necessary.

Mr. Ratz said that the Examiners had been impressed by the CDTI's rapidity of response and advisory capacity. Businessmen would like it to provide subsidies too, but this was contrary to its doctrine. Mr. Ratz argued that such subsidies were not outright grants, since they had a multiplier effect and were, in fact, an investment that was certainly of benefit to the country as a whole.

Mrs. Verdeja said that MINER's policy thrust had indeed changed. Although the modernisation of several ailing industries was not yet complete, many objectives had already been achieved, so that some funds were now available to promote new industries and the introduction of new technologies (e.g. computers, robotics, energy saving) in existing industries. A distinction must therefore be made between targeted operations and the more general dissemination of knowledge to the 5 000 or so SMEs, which could benefit by recent advances. Hence the development of a consultancy network providing them with not only technological advice but also assistance with management, quality control and product design, sometimes related to standardization.

Mrs. Verdeja did not want the CDTI's role to be confused with that of the venture capital companies, for which much had been done, notably with the creation of the second market in Madrid and Barcelona. She also had reserves about the CDTI's granting subsidies. Subsidies should be avoided when an operation was closely market-related, though they might be justified at the project definition stage.

The Spanish tax system was unsophisticated and needed to be improved. At present tax incentives were ineffective compared with the United States system. Concessional loans would be preferable. Spain did, however, offer tax incentives in one instance, i.e. to venture capital companies.

Some sectoral plans were then described:

- The electronics and computerisation plan, which included a chapter on government procurement;
- The plan for the pharmaceutical industries, which should have their own technological development capacity within the next five years. Public and private sectors must step up their research and their co-operation;
- The energy research plan, which covered a number of points:
  - More efficient use of electricity;
  - Improved coal combustion;
  - Nuclear energy; and
  - The different renewable energies (including the use of small-scale power plants and biomass).

Co-operative research in this sector was unique in that while the electricity companies were private (though with some government participation), it was the government that set the price of electricity and included in it a component specifically earmarked for the funding of the kind of co-operative research managed jointly within the framework of OCIDE programmes.

Industry in Spain, which had previously been highly protected and not especially forward-looking, had adjusted successfully. The importation of technology would now be more selective, and joint ventures with foreign firms would be encouraged. This implied crossborder mobility for researchers, and financing would be available to encourage that mobility. SMEs formed the backbone of Spanish industry and would receive additional aid from the CDTI, but there would obviously be no question of doubling this at autonomous community level. Such aid was essentially a national tool.

Mr. Ratz said that the system of tax benefits for R&D had the serious disadvantage of being difficult to control at Ministry of Finance level.

Mr. Larsson (Sweden) said that tax incentives to encourage industrial research had been phased out in his country, but this had not prevented R&D expenditure from growing. *Mr. Koskenlinna* (Finland) emphasized the financial requirements of industry and asked for information on Spain's participation in EUREKA. This issue was to be discussed next.

IV. THE ROLE OF UNIVERSITIES AND PUBLIC RESEARCH INSTITUTIONS

This topic was introduced by *Mr. Piganiol*. University research, in crisis in so many countries, was inseparable from university teaching in that it helped academics to progress, to understand and to explain. It needed to be free and untrammelled.

For the advancement of knowledge, however, it was necessary that there should be, side by side with this fruitful but unco-ordinated research, structured centres employing large teams of researchers and fully equipped to carry out programmes carefully planned to advance science as a whole and to take account of other factors, too – especially economic factors.

In most countries funds for basic research were increasingly being allocated to these centres, causing some bitterness in the universities, and all the more so because their own credits often came either from such centres, (as in France where CNRS programmes include some university research) or from specialist institutions whose criteria were sometimes very strict.

In fact, academics were now so numerous that it was impossible to fund research by all of them. A distinction had to be made between higher education (whose vocation is to advance the frontiers of knowledge, which needs to engage in original research, and is thoroughly able to do so), and other post-secondary school higher education (whose function is to transmit well-established findings and whose main requirement is to be able to conduct experiments).

The question therefore was, what line was Spain to follow in this respect, now and in the future?

It was, moreover, becoming impossible for even large research establishments to encompass all the specialities involved in the assignments entrusted to them. They had to be able to contract work outside, for instance to the universities – as, indeed, they often did already. But there must also be some incentive for them to do so; it could be very tempting for them to hold on to as many funds as possible for their intramural research. How was this difficulty to be overcome?

Mr. Munoz, Director of Science Policy, first spoke of the past role of the CSIC, set up in 1939, and the action of the CAICYT, which had been open-handed in its response to justified requests, so that the universities had been freely funded.

Infrastructure, however, was inadequate and appropriations had dwindled. By 1978, only 10 per cent of CSIC budget was available for the operational side, the remainder being taken up by staffing and administration costs.

Recently considerable efforts had been made to renovate infrastructure (with expenditures of Ptas 8 billion extra in the last four years) and to increase the CSIC budget.

Mr. Munoz stressed three points:

- First, universities should be able to supplement their budget by obtaining grants from industry or the regions;

- Researcher mobility was very important. A decree to be enacted shortly should improve that mobility and allow research institutions to recruit foreigners and perhaps, eventually, offer them permanent posts;
- Provision had been made in the National Plan for work to be contracted out by the research institutions where desirable. The terms of such contracts had been specified in the Act.

Lastly, academics could now work with the CSIC. Some 32 agreements had been signed with the universities.

Mr. Marcum, citing the case of IBM, which would be needing 26 000 well-trained young people, said this example showed how important it was for the universities to watch the market closely and respond to its demands.

Mr. Munoz knew there was a training bottleneck. Studies were in hand to reform curricula and diversify post-secondary education right up to doctorate level. Eighteen committees comprising academics and representatives of labour and management had been meeting for that purpose. Reform, however, would take time. The proportion of human sciences doctorates, for example, had been reduced to 33 per cent in 1983, against 45 per cent in 1982; but to continue in this direction adequate training potential was required, and Spain had no hesitation in having recourse to international resources.

Mr. Denozios (Greece) said that in many areas the borderline between fundamental and applied research was very vague. He cited the example of materials, and expressed the fear that in creating an institute to study that field Greece might be subsidising work that other countries would exploit and develop. What could be done to protect university R&D results?

Replying, *Mr. Munoz* said this was a very serious problem when a country did not have its own industrial fabric in the sector concerned. It was hoped that patents legislation would provide a solution. But he thought that protection alone was not enough. Steps to obtain the best returns on research must also be taken.

V. INTERNATIONAL CO-OPERATION

This item, hardly mentioned by the Examiners, had been put on the agenda at the request of Spain, whose R&D policy encompassed its European co-operation effort.

Mr. Marcum, in introducing the topic, emphasized that product development concerned all the OECD countries. Flows of products, services and information were considerable. Every day some five billion manufactures and one billion services were traded. Products based on new technologies now accounted for one-quarter to one-third of all trade in goods. Nearly half of all investment was in new technology. More and more licences were being paid for. Product life was shorter. All this applied in Spain too. And while competition was fiercer, at the same time international co-operation was being stepped up.

Referring to the many European co-operation projects, Mr. Marcum noted that Spain was already involved in several EUREKA projects, and that private companies co-operated more readily and more successfully than governments, perhaps because government co-operation usually concerned difficult large-scale projects.

Spain was in a good position to co-operate successfully in that it had a liberal tradition of research and technology transfers. There was every reason to hope that Spain would play a growing part in the development of European scale operations.

Mrs. Verdeja thanked Mr. Marcum for his contribution to the debate. She was aware of the importance of this topic added to the agenda by Spain. Spanish institutions ought to take part in international projects, and information on current and future projects should be circulated freely. Spain would naturally expect a fair technical and industrial return in exchange for its financial contributions.

Spain contributed 3 per cent (or Ptas 5 billion) of the budget of the European Space Agency (ESA), and was a member of the European Organisation for Nuclear Research (CERN). Obviously, it expected a return in terms of scientific and technical knowledge. In the past the use made of the funds paid to ESA had been checked by the Spanish Space Institute, but the new legislation stipulated that to ensure a coherent policy all co-operative budgets should in future be monitored by the Interministerial Commission. It was hoped that Spanish industry and research centres would play a greater role in European projects.

The same question arose as concerned CERN, whose activity was essentially scientific and to which Spain contributed Ptas 2.3 billion. It was hoped that here, too, participation by Spanish researchers would be increased.

Spain's participation in the EUREKA projects, a very interesting component of Spanish policy, was to be stepped up. Spain currently took part in 14 projects (and was leader in 6). It was hoped shortly to increase the number of projects in which it took part to 24 (representing a total contribution of Ptas 20 billion). The CDTI was to be strengthened so that it could administer Spanish participation in the EUREKA projects, and Spain would be presiding the organisation for the first nine month of 1987.

Spain hoped that its European experience would also give it a better understanding of the social changes that would be brought about by new technologies.

Spain took part in the EEC Framework Programme and was especially interested in biotechnology, the BRITE project and non-nuclear energy resources; it had submitted 50 projects. It had also concluded bilateral agreements on other projects, e.g. those in which the Almeria Solar Plant took part.

Mr. Esteban Delas (Germany) regretted that the Examiners' Report did not contain a chapter on this topic. These regrets were shared by *Mr. Paillon* (EEC), especially as Spain's entry into the Common Market justified such a study. He did not entirely agree with Mr. Marcum that companies would be readier than governments to take part in co-operative operations. That might be true of large corporations, but did not apply to small and medium-sized enterprises.

Nevertheless, interest on the part of SMEs was growing much more quickly in Spain than in other countries. Interested firms were hoping for more financial and moral support from their government. Support might also take the form of information, standardization, wider market openings and venture capital – naturally with due regard for the rules of competition.

Mrs. Verdeja replied that finance was not the prime concern of Spanish firms; nor was there any fund in Spain for EUREKA. Most of the firms co-operating were SMEs seeking international contacts and wider markets. EUREKA offered a very effective framework for international business communication; certain projects, however, required specific standardization or certification measures. Spain had set up the AENOR, a private association receiving some financial support from MINER.

Firms were asking for freer access to government contracts. This question was being studied. It would be of great importance in 1992.

Spain had put the accent hitherto on assimilation of technologies. While this must continue, domestic innovation potential must also be developed.

Mr. Denozios (Greece) noted the mention in the report of "technology registers" such as existed in Latin America (although there they appeared to be bureaucratically filtered). Could they not be improved so as to serve as guides for firms?

Mrs. Verdeja said these registers had been established originally as a means of foreign exchange and payments control, not to inventory technologies. Their character was changing, and they already provided valuable information on the technologies exported and imported.

VI. CONCLUSIONS

Mr. Munoz thanked the Examiners for their work. There had been agreement on most points, and where there were disagreements, these had been thoroughly discussed and explained at the review meeting, which had been very satisfactory.

At the end of this review exercise, one thing was clear. Spain's R&D and innovation policy was developing fast. The field of experience was in many ways so exciting that it would be a pity to wait for years before looking again at the progress made. Regular monitoring would be rewarding for all concerned, as the Examiners agreed. It was to be hoped that the exercise could be repeated soon.

Annex

LIST OF PARTICIPANTS

Chairman: Mrs. Kerstin Eliasson,
Head of Divison, Ministry of Education and
Cultural Affairs, Stockholm, Sweden

Examiners

Mr. Pierre Piganiol,
Rapporteur, Former Délégué
à la Recherche,
France.

Mr. Konrad Ratz,
Director, Fund for Research Promotion,
Vienna, Austria.

Mr. Benjamin Huberman,
Former Deputy Director of the Office for
Scientific and Technological Policy,
Washington DC, United States.

SPANISH DELEGATION

Mr. J.M. Rojo
Secretary of State
for the Universities and Research

Mr. M.A. Feito
Under-Secretary for Industry and Energy

Mrs. I. Verdeja Lizama
Director-General for Industrial
Innovation and Technology (MINER)

Mr. E. Munoz
Director of Science Policy (MEC)

Mr. E. Trillas
Chairman of the Higher Council
for Scientific Research (CSIC)

Mr. J. Sebastian
Vice-Chairman of the Higher Council for
Scientific Research (CSIC)

Mr. E. Tortosa
Vice-Chairman of the Higher Council
for Scientific Research (CSIC)

Mr. J. Gil Pelaez
Deputy Director for Industrial
Innovation and Technology (MINER)

Mr. J.M. Isac
Ministry of Industry and Energy

Mr. I. Egea
Ministry of Industry and Energy

Mr. J. Antonio Fuertes
Ministry of Industry and Energy

Mr. C. Navarro
CSTP Delegate for the Ministry of
Education and Science

Mr. I. Fernandez de Lucio
Director of the Planning Office
of the CSIC

Mr. A. Rebollo
IMPI

Mr. A. Cadenas Marin
CSTP Delegate for the Ministry of
Education and Science

Mrs. P. Sanchez
CSTP Delegate for the Ministry of
Industry and Energy

Mrs. S. Meca
Secretary-General of the CSIC

Mr. J. Ruiz
Counsellor, Spanish Delegation to the
OECD

OTHER SCIENTIFIC AND TECHNOLOGICAL POLICY
COMMITTEE DELEGATES

Mr. M. Koskenlinna,
Finland

Mr. Ph. Barré,
France

Mrs. M. Lamouroux,
France

Mr. D. Deniozos,
Greece

Mrs. L. Enriques,
Portugal

Mr. F. Goncalves,
Portugal

Mr. C. Malmborg,
Sweden

Mr. P. Smith,
United Kingdom

Mr. M. Paillon
EEC

Mr. J.P. Meullenet,
France

Mr. Carsalade,
France

Mr. J. Esteban Delas,
Germany

Mrs. M. Travers,
Ireland

Mr. F. Bello,
Portugal

Mr. G. Larsson,
Sweden

Mr. P. Landelius,
Sweden

Mrs. S. Vlaeminck,
EEC

OECD SECRETARIAT

Mr. J.M. Marcum,
Director for Science, Technology and Industry

Mr. J.D. Bell,
Head of the Science and Technology Policy Division

Mrs. M. Solanes

WHERE TO OBTAIN OECD PUBLICATIONS
OÙ OBTENIR LES PUBLICATIONS DE L'OCDE

ARGENTINA - ARGENTINE
Carlos Hirsch S.R.L.,
Florida 165, 4º Piso,
(Galeria Guemes) 1333 Buenos Aires
Tel. 33.1787.2391 y 30.7122

AUSTRALIA - AUSTRALIE
D.A. Book (Aust.) Pty. Ltd.
11-13 Station Street (P.O. Box 163)
Mitcham, Vic. 3132   Tel. (03) 873 4411

AUSTRIA - AUTRICHE
OECD Publications and Information Centre,
4 Simrockstrasse,
5300 Bonn (Germany)   Tel. (0228) 21.60.45
Gerold & Co., Graben 31, Wien 1 Tel. 52.22.35

BELGIUM - BELGIQUE
Jean de Lannoy,
avenue du Roi 202
B-1060 Bruxelles   Tel. (02) 538.51.69

CANADA
Renouf Publishing Company Ltd/
Éditions Renouf Ltée,
1294 Algoma Road, Ottawa, Ont. K1B 3W8
Tel: (613) 741-4333
Toll Free/Sans Frais:
Ontario, Quebec, Maritimes:
1-800-267-1805
Western Canada, Newfoundland:
1-800-267-1826
Stores/Magasins:
61 rue Sparks St., Ottawa, Ont. K1P 5A6
Tel: (613) 238-8985
211 rue Yonge St., Toronto, Ont. M5B 1M4
Tel: (416) 363-3171

DENMARK - DANEMARK
Munksgaard Export and Subscription Service
35, Nørre Søgade, DK-1370 København K
Tel. +45.1.12.85.70

FINLAND - FINLANDE
Akateeminen Kirjakauppa,
Keskuskatu 1, 00100 Helsinki 10 Tel. 0.12141

FRANCE
OCDE/OECD
Mail Orders/Commandes par correspondance :
2, rue André-Pascal,
75775 Paris Cedex 16
Tel. (1) 45.24.82.00
Bookshop/Librairie : 33, rue Octave-Feuillet
75016 Paris
Tel. (1) 45.24.81.67 or/ou (1) 45.24.81.81
Librairie de l'Université,
12a, rue Nazareth,
13602 Aix-en-Provence   Tel. 42.26.18.08

GERMANY - ALLEMAGNE
OECD Publications and Information Centre,
4 Simrockstrasse,
5300 Bonn   Tel. (0228) 21.60.45

GREECE - GRÈCE
Librairie Kauffmann,
28, rue du Stade, 105 64 Athens Tel. 322.21.60

HONG KONG
Government Information Services,
Publications (Sales) Office,
Information Services Department
No. 1, Battery Path, Central

ICELAND - ISLANDE
Snæbjörn Jónsson & Co., h.f.,
Hafnarstræti 4 & 9,
P.O.B. 1131 – Reykjavik
Tel. 13133/14281/11936

INDIA - INDE
Oxford Book and Stationery Co.,
Scindia House, New Delhi 1 Tel. 331.5896/5308
17 Park St., Calcutta 700016   Tel. 240832

INDONESIA - INDONÉSIE
Pdii-Lipi, P.O. Box 3065/JKT.Jakarta
Tel. 583467

IRELAND - IRLANDE
TDC Publishers - Library Suppliers,
12 North Frederick Street, Dublin 1
Tel. 744835-749677

ITALY - ITALIE
Libreria Commissionaria Sansoni,
Via Lamarmora 45, 50121 Firenze
Tel. 579751/584468
Via Bartolini 29, 20155 Milano   Tel. 365083
Editrice e Libreria Herder,
Piazza Montecitorio 120, 00186 Roma
Tel. 6794628
Libreria Hœpli,
Via Hœpli 5, 20121 Milano   Tel. 865446
Libreria Scientifica
Dott. Lucio de Biasio "Aeiou"
Via Meravigli 16, 20123 Milano   Tel. 807679
Libreria Lattes,
Via Garibaldi 3, 10122 Torino   Tel. 519274
La diffusione delle edizioni OCSE è inoltre
assicurata dalle migliori librerie nelle città più
importanti.

JAPAN - JAPON
OECD Publications and Information Centre,
Landic Akasaka Bldg., 2-3-4 Akasaka,
Minato-ku, Tokyo 107   Tel. 586.2016

KOREA - CORÉE
Kyobo Book Centre Co. Ltd.
P.O.Box: Kwang Hwa Moon 1658,
Seoul   Tel. (REP) 730.78.91

LEBANON - LIBAN
Documenta Scientifica/Redico,
Edison Building, Bliss St.,
P.O.B. 5641, Beirut   Tel. 354429-344425

MALAYSIA - MALAISIE
University of Malaya Co-operative Bookshop
Ltd.,
P.O.Box 1127, Jalan Pantai Baru,
Kuala Lumpur   Tel. 577701/577072

NETHERLANDS - PAYS-BAS
Staatsuitgeverij
Chr. Plantijnstraat, 2 Postbus 20014
2500 EA S-Gravenhage   Tel. 070-789911
Voor bestellingen: Tel. 070-789880

NEW ZEALAND - NOUVELLE-ZÉLANDE
Government Printing Office Bookshops:
Auckland: Retail Bookshop, 25 Rutland Stseet,
Mail Orders, 85 Beach Road
Private Bag C.P.O.
Hamilton: Retail: Ward Street,
Mail Orders, P.O. Box 857
Wellington: Retail, Mulgrave Street, (Head
Office)
Cubacade World Trade Centre,
Mail Orders, Private Bag
Christchurch: Retail, 159 Hereford Street,
Mail Orders, Private Bag
Dunedin: Retail, Princes Street,
Mail Orders, P.O. Box 1104

NORWAY - NORVÈGE
Tanum-Karl Johan
Karl Johans gate 43, Oslo 1
PB 1177 Sentrum, 0107 Oslo 1Tel. (02) 42.93.10

PAKISTAN
Mirza Book Agency
65 Shahrah Quaid-E-Azam, Lahore 3 Tel. 66839

PORTUGAL
Livraria Portugal,
Rua do Carmo 70-74, 1117 Lisboa Codex
Tel. 360582/3

SINGAPORE - SINGAPOUR
Information Publications Pte Ltd
Pei-Fu Industrial Building,
24 New Industrial Road No. 02-06
Singapore 1953   Tel. 2831786, 2831798

SPAIN - ESPAGNE
Mundi-Prensa Libros, S.A.,
Castelló 37, Apartado 1223, Madrid-28001
Tel. 431.33.99
Libreria Bosch, Ronda Universidad 11,
Barcelona 7   Tel. 317.53.08/317.53.58

SWEDEN - SUÈDE
AB CE Fritzes Kungl. Hovbokhandel,
Box 16356, S 103 27 STH,
DS Stockholm   Tel. (08) 23.89.00
Subscription Agency/Abonnements:
Wennergren-Williams AB,
Box 30004, S104 25 Stockholm Tel. (08)54.12.00

SWITZERLAND - SUISSE
OECD Publications and Information Centre,
4 Simrockstrasse,
5300 Bonn (Germany)   Tel. (0228) 21.60.45
Librairie Payot,
6 rue Grenus, 1211 Genève 11
Tel. (022) 31.89.50
United Nations Bookshop/
Librairie des Nations-Unies
Palais des Nations,
1211 – Geneva 10
Tel. 022-34-60-11 (ext. 48 72)

TAIWAN - FORMOSE
Good Faith Worldwide Int'l Co., Ltd.
9th floor, No. 118, Sec.2
Chung Hsiao E. Road
Taipei   Tel. 391.7396/391.7397

THAILAND - THAILANDE
Suksit Siam Co., Ltd.,
1715 Rama IV Rd.,
Samyam Bangkok 5   Tel. 2511630

TURKEY - TURQUIE
Kültur Yayinlari Is-Türk Ltd. Sti.
Atatürk Bulvari No: 191/Kat. 21
Kavaklidere/Ankara   Tel. 25.07.60
Dolmabahce Cad. No: 29
Besiktas/Istanbul   Tel. 160.71.88

UNITED KINGDOM - ROYAUME-UNI
H.M. Stationery Office,
Postal orders only: (01)211-5656
P.O.B. 276, London SW8 5DT
Telephone orders: (01) 622.3316, or
Personal callers:
49 High Holborn, London WC1V 6HB
Branches at: Belfast, Birmingham,
Bristol, Edinburgh, Manchester

UNITED STATES - ÉTATS-UNIS
OECD Publications and Information Centre,
2001 L Street, N.W., Suite 700,
Washington, D.C. 20036 - 4095
Tel. (202) 785.6323

VENEZUELA
Libreria del Este,
Avda F. Miranda 52, Aptdo. 60337,
Edificio Galipan, Caracas 106
Tel. 32.23.01/33.26.04/31.58.38

YUGOSLAVIA - YOUGOSLAVIE
Jugoslovenska Knjiga, Knez Mihajlova 2,
P.O.B. 36, Beograd   Tel. 621.992

Orders and inquiries from countries where
Distributors have not yet been appointed should be
sent to:
OECD, Publications Service, Sales and
Distribution Division, 2, rue André-Pascal, 75775
PARIS CEDEX 16.

Les commandes provenant de pays où l'OCDE n'a
pas encore désigné de distributeur peuvent être
adressées à :
OCDE, Service des Publications. Division des
Ventes et Distribution. 2. rue André-Pascal. 75775
PARIS CEDEX 16.

71055-09-1987

OECD PUBLICATIONS, 2, rue André-Pascal, 75775 PARIS CEDEX 16 - No. 44193 1987
PRINTED IN FRANCE
(92 87 06 1) ISBN 92-64-13029-2